THE BRIDGE

Restoration and the Way Back Home

DARIO L. PERLA

WESTBOW
PRESS®
A DIVISION OF THOMAS NELSON
& ZONDERVAN

WestBow Press books may be ordered through booksellers or by contacting:

WestBow Press
A Division of Thomas Nelson & Zondervan
1663 Liberty Drive
Bloomington, IN 47403
www.westbowpress.com
1 (866) 928-1240

All Scripture quotations, unless otherwise indicated, are taken from the Holy Bible, New International Version®, NIV®. Copyright ©1973, 1978, 1984, 2011 by Biblica, Inc.™ Used by permission of Zondervan. All rights reserved worldwide. www.zondervan.com The "NIV" and "New International Version" are trademarks registered in the United States Patent and Trademark Office by Biblica, Inc.™

Scripture quotations marked (NASB) taken from the New American Standard Bible® (NASB), Copyright © 1960, 1962, 1963, 1968, 1971, 1972, 1973, 1975, 1977, 1995 by The Lockman Foundation Used by permission. www.Lockman.org"

Scripture quotations marked (KJV) are from the King James Version of the Bible.

ISBN: 978-1-9736-6815-2 (sc)
ISBN: 978-1-9736-6816-9 (hc)
ISBN: 978-1-9736-6814-5 (e)

Library of Congress Control Number: 2019911247

Print information available on the last page.

WestBow Press rev. date: 08/26/2019

CONTENTS

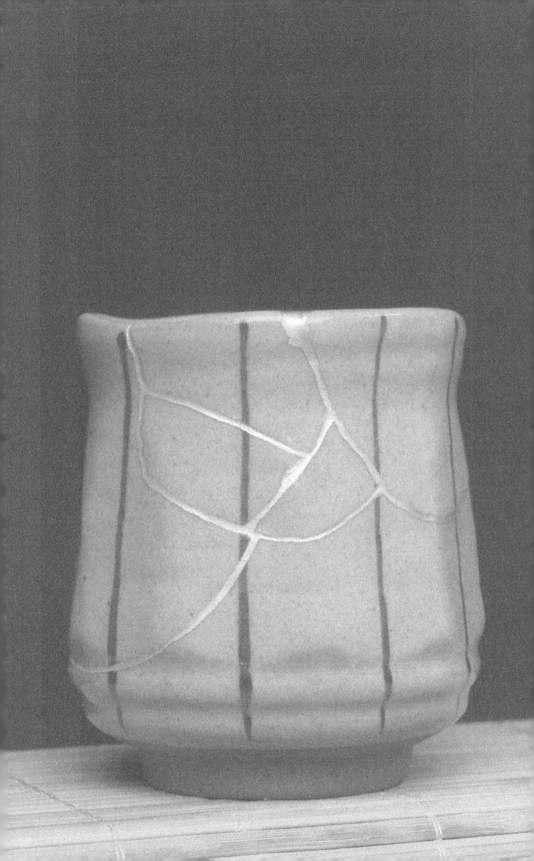

Kintsukuroi

(n.) (v. phr) "to repair with gold"; the art of repairing pottery with gold or silver lacquer and understanding that the piece is more beautiful for having been broken

THE JOURNEY

I have heard it said all my life; enjoy the journey! Enjoy the ride! Put together; Life is a journey so enjoy the ride! And the always popular; Remember, it's the journey that counts not the destination! Plus many more, but what do they mean? Have you ever stopped to just let quotes like these ruminate in your mind and then begin to unpack them? I do all the time. It's because I'm a thinker and that's what thinkers do.

So when I was called to write my book and was informed that it would be a seven year journey I naturally looked at the beginning and the end. I believe its human nature. What would life be like when I finish? What will I be like when I finish? Will I have arrived? But I've heard it said many times before; you never really arrive! So I ask the question; if life is a journey, and it's the journey that counts, why beginnings and endings? I could ask a hundred more questions but I'd rather look for answers.

In the later part of my seven year journey to the garden while writing the book I started to realize that what I was experiencing during this time resembled Psalm 23. It was during the time God began to heal and restore my emotions. As I read the words of Psalm 23 I constantly saw many similarities to my journey and the one King David had written about. I was experiencing the same emotions, feelings and thoughts as him. I was also encountering the struggles and hardships he mentioned, as well as the deliverance from them. I would actually say to myself often, "I feel as if I am on a Psalm 23 journey."

I started to realize King David and I were on the same path but in different times on earth; He was Old Testament, I am New Testament. They are two completely different dispensations, in other words two times in life when God related to people in different ways. David didn't know who Jesus was but he believed God said He was coming and lived in faith to that promise. I know Jesus personally because He died for me 2000 years ago and gave me His Spirit as a guarantee for eternity, just as David's faith gave him a guarantee for eternity. We both believed God but from opposite sides of the cross. The beauty here is the dichotomy of our faiths produced the exact same experience; a Psalm 23 journey.

So that got me thinking, if God has two of His children experience the exact same journey but in completely different eras, it must be the journey that matters and not the destination because King David and I are not going to end up in the same place here on earth. He was born 3000 years before I was. We will end up at the same destination in eternity, just not here on earth. So my ultimate conclusion is that it is the journey that counts and here's why.

God's ultimate purpose in allowing us to experience the Psalm 23 journey is to bring us back home. To restore our souls and lead us to the best possible life we can live here on earth. To bring us back to the garden, our original paradise abode. That's what restoration means; the action of returning something to a former owner (God), place (Garden) or original condition (Wholeness). And it is in the journey that God can change the condition of our lives from that of a wasteland to one of a garden as He restores the landscapes of our hearts from weeds to fruit bearing plants and from lies to truth. **The journey is not about arriving, it is about becoming!**

Now the journey is starting to make more sense. In the very early years of my new life in Christ, about 22 years ago or so, I was sitting on the ledge of a mountain top in West Texas praying to God about my future and my desire to serve Him will all of my being. I reached a point in our one way talk, my way, in which I laid my life plans out to God. My plans were to leave my career and go to seminary; after that change the world. I was then so gracious as to ask God for His opinion. Well I got it! God flat out said to me in a stern but loving voice, "Those are not my plans for you. You are to stay in your career and start your own business which I would appreciate if you named after me. (Which I did, "Master's Apparel") And then let me take it from there. Remember Dario, it's not what you do for a living, it's who you are that counts!" Wow!!! Little did I know that 15 years prior to my brokenness and the seven year Psalm 23 journey I took back home to the garden that God initiated the process in my soul by His words on that mountain top. That's Jeremiah 29:11 coming to life, "For I know the plans

I have for you," declares the Lord, "plans to prosper you and not to harm you, plans to give you hope and a future." God already has your Psalm 23 journey planned for you and it will absolutely lead to the best possible life you can live here on earth! It's 100% God guaranteed!

So come walk alongside me on my seven year journey as we cross an amazing bridge from the wasteland back home to the garden. I pray it will encourage you to embark on your own personal journey to the very best life possible; the one God already has planned for you!

PSALM 23

(1)The Lord is my shepherd, I shall not be in want.
(2)He makes me lie down in green pastures,
he leads me besides quiet waters,
(3)He restores my soul. He guides me in the paths
of righteousness for his name's sake.
(4)Even though I walk through the valley of the shadow of death, I will
fear no evil, for you are with me; your rod and your staff, they comfort me.
(5)You prepare a table before me in the presence of my
enemies. You anoint my head with oil; my cup over flows.
(6)Surely goodness and love will follow me all the days of my
life, and I will dwell in the house of the Lord forever.

BROKENNESS IS THE BRIDGE
Year One

The bridge of brokenness is a bridge that brings one to the end of one's self. It is a gift from God. It sets you free from the lies of an Enemy that wants to keep you in bondage and leads you on a journey to discover the truth that will set you free from the fears those lies produce. It leads to a life lived in a garden where freedom from fear is the norm, not the exception. It can be a somewhat brutal journey, arduous at times, but worth every second due to its final destination. It involves a life of total reliance on and complete surrender to God. It is an internal journey that will challenge one down to the very core of who you are. It is a journey that all are called to but few will answer. But to those who answer the call the rewards are divine and last for eternity.

My journey to the bridge of brokenness reached its peak on April 21, 2007. At eight o'clock that morning my phone rang and the words 'mom's cell' appeared on the caller I.D. I instantly knew something was wrong. My brother was on the other end of the call, and in a broken voice said that our niece had been in a car accident, broke her neck and was paralyzed from the neck down". I felt my heart fall to the floor. After what seemed like an eternity, I caught my breath and started thinking about being with her. Unfortunately, I was on a fishing trip in Ardmore, OK hundreds of miles from home in Atlanta and where she was in Florida with no quick and easy way to get back. I was helpless, and knew it. At this point I had a choice to make. I could lean on God and trust in His plan, or take things into my own hands and fight this battle for Him. Although I thought I chose the former like 'every good Christian' should, I would come to realize that I actually choose the latter. It was the beginning of my end.

It was here that I decided to become the spiritual giant I desired to be and take on the Enemy in my own strength and defeat him for God. Once I made it back to Atlanta from Florida, where my niece and immediate family members would spend the next six months at a spinal recovery center, I started introducing Christ and my new life in him to them at every opportunity that presented itself. I wanted them to see just how much of a warrior for God I had become. Deep down in my heart I thought it was my time to shine for the Lord!

I spent countless hours with my niece at the Spinal Recovery Center over the next several months, deeply concerned about her spiritual, emotional and physical state. Two months into her recovery our conversations had become very deep to the point where she was willing to consider salvation in Jesus. One Tuesday evening, after convincing a dear friend and mentor to accompany me to the Center, all three of us prayed together as she accepted Jesus as Lord and Savior. It was one of the greatest joys of my life. And, it went straight to my head! I remember driving home that evening full of pride and thinking "I am on fire for God". Seconds later I grabbed the steering wheel with tightly clenched fists, looked out into the world and uttered my most infamous words, "Is that all you have Satan?!!! Now I am coming after you!" I didn't fully know at the time but at that very moment the battle had begun. The battle for control of my soul unleashed like never before. Though I could not see it, the bridge of brokenness appeared before me and my journey to it was drawing closer. I had reached the pinnacle of my pride in self.

THE VALLEY OF ACHOR

The journey of brokenness and restoration starts by God bringing us to a place we all know but don't care to go: the wilderness, the valley of Achor. In the book of Hosea, Chapter 2:14-15, God speaks through the prophet Hosea when He tells of His plans to restore the Jewish people back to His favor. "Therefore, behold I will allure her, bring her into the wilderness and speak kindly to her. Then I will give her back her vineyards, and will make the valley of Achor a door of hope". These verses outline the plan God has for those He is leading to the end of their self-life, a life apart from

Himself. He brings us out into the wilderness by alluring us, romancing us to a place where we feel as if we are all alone and gives us trouble, trials and tribulations. But in His wisdom He knows this valley will become a door of hope to those who persevere and will lead us to the life He has for us. It is there in the valley of Achor (trouble) where He gently begins to speak to our hearts as He draws us into His Life for us.

And trouble it was! Though I had been experiencing many hardships for the past 13 years of my new life in Christ, this is where God turned up the heat and the wheels really began to fall off of my self-life. I had trouble in every area of my life. It was the end of the longest summer I had ever experienced. I had just spent the past 5 months helping my sister and niece get through their stay at the Spinal Center. I was exhausted in every way but vowed to re-energize and continue my war against the Enemy. For the next two years I fought and struggled through troubles - one after another. In that period I had nine friends and family members pass away. I totaled my car in an accident, escaping with my life only to have the first of three surgeries I would need over the next twenty four months. I also had two trips to the emergency room, one straight from the airport that lead to an excruciating double root canal. The economy tanked and I began to lose clients by the handful wondering if I would even have a custom clothing career when it was all said and done.

I finally realized in a physical way that I was deep into the wilderness when I was lying on my bed one summer afternoon in 2008. I had a splint on my pinky that I broke during the car accident. It was to help straighten the tendon after surgery. My right shoulder was in a sling, recovering from bone spur surgery a few weeks back. I also had my foot in a stretching boot after several injections of cortisone to help it heal from a severe case of planter fasciitis. I remember thinking, "I'm in trouble, my entire body is breaking down with no relief in sight, and God is nowhere to be found." Over the next year I sank deeper and deeper into the darkness of the self-life. I would soon realize I was in deep trouble spiritually as well. I woke up to have quiet time with God, only to discover I was totally alone. I looked out the window of my bedroom into a beautifully bright, August morning and saw nothing but dark skies. I looked for God and He was gone, along with His warmth. I knelt there ice cold wondering where He was and thought to myself, "Where did He go? And how did I get here?"

I now realize God had lured (romanced) me into the wilderness and was gently guiding me through the valley of Achor (trouble) before bringing me to a gate, the 'door of hope'. I fought hard not to enter that door and hold onto my self-life. It was the only life I had ever known. I sought escape in every direction to not enter that door. I even contemplated putting my house up for sale and moving to Wilmington, NC where I could hide from God's plan for my life! I was just so scared to leave the wasteland where I was living for my entire life. One filled with pain, loneliness, drama and a whole lot of selfishness! It was all I ever knew and it was comfortable. But God's love for me was overwhelming and He stopped that move as fast as it began. Then, after a few deeply destructive dating relationships, I began to realize that my time in the wasteland was over! Living life on my own terms wasn't working anymore, and it was coming to an end!

I awoke one morning in January 2010 as alone as I have ever felt. I was in the depths of despair and realized I was broken! I had finally reached the end of my rope, the end of myself. My desire to do life my way (self-will) was broken. That's what brokenness is: God breaking our will to do life our way so He can once and for all lead us by His perfect will to our best life possible!

While I was sitting there alone in the pit of brokenness, I saw the door. It was then that I chose to walk through the door of hope. The choice of living life my own way had finally become more painful than surrendering it to God. But I still had to choose. No one can walk through the door of hope unless they choose to do so. Love is a choice and I was about to get a second chance at love and here's why! God's gentleness will lead us through the wilderness right up to the door, but we must choose to enter. And when we do, the exchange takes place. Our life for His! Luke 17:33 says it beautifully; "Whoever tries to keep his life will lose it, and whoever loses his life will preserve it"; and there I was, through the door of hope and on my knees in a state of brokenness!

TWO CHOICES

Before we discuss a way out of the wasteland I want to share with you my testimony about how I became a Christian and the two ultimate choices we all will face in this life. Ever since I was young, maybe 3 years old, I have sensed that something was wrong. Inside I felt as if I was destined for paradise and that life should be a moment by moment glimpse of that paradise where everything is perfect and every moment is bliss. Eternal paradise is what my heart yearned for. God set this desire in my heart when he knit me together in my mother's womb. But after I was born and could put my thoughts together, I realized my inside and my outside didn't match up. Something was wrong! What my heart desired and what my senses experienced where not lining up. I desired peace, but there was chaos. I desired relationship, but there was strife. I desired constant love, but there were times of abandonment. I desired acceptance, but felt rejected at times. What is going on?!!!

It wasn't long before I found myself retreating into a cave all by myself and calling a time out. "I don't like it out there!" was my prominent thought. "I wonder if I can live in here where I feel safe." And so began my life lived all alone in a cave in the back corner of a wasteland where I was never meant to live in the first place. Although it was a lonely existence for 29 years, I still had this sense that there was a way out, that there was this beacon of light and the end of this long dark tunnel leading out of the wasteland. This longing to see that light is what kept me going the whole time I was in that cave. Then, at the age of 29 I received a knock on the door to my heart and decided to answer it.

It was a night in August of 1994 while sitting at home watching television that I was asked to make the first of two choices. But that night I had a dilemma, "How was I going to watch television without any dope (marijuana)?" I hated watching television without being high; but that night I had no choice. So I began my sober channel surfing quest and somehow I came across a Christian television network I had seen my dad watch in the last years of his life. A channel he begged me to watch with him with no luck. I wasn't about to get suckered in by those crazy religious folks and refused his offer every time. But my curiosity got the best of me that night and I decided to just see what could have possibly had my father's attention. I began watching the program and within 10 minutes I was amazed how it was as if the speaker was talking directly to me. A few minutes later the speaker invites all in attendance who want to receive the gift of salvation to get out of their seats and come down front for prayer. He then looks out into the camera and invites those who are at home to come kneel before the television and pray to receive the gift of salvation. That was me; I'm thinking I finally found a way out of the cave! Needless to say I was freaked out though. I couldn't believe what was happening; it seemed to come out of nowhere. I literally ran around to shut all the blinds in the room so nobody could see me. I felt like I was on Candid Camera, and somebody was filming my reaction to this prank! It was crazy! But something inside of me said this is it, the choice my heart wanted to make ever since I could remember. Saying yes to God's free gift of salvation could straighten what was crooked in me. This decision would give me hope for the first time in life and allow me re-entry back into my intended paradise garden home; no more living in a cave in the wasteland. But the choice to accept Jesus as my Lord and Savior was only the first of two choices I would need to say yes to.

So after saying yes to Jesus and the gift of eternal salvation I was confronted with a second choice; Do I choose to say yes to the surrendering of my new found life to God and His process of sanctification (changing us from the inside out), or do I do it on my own and go it alone (change from the outside in)? This decision to say yes to sanctification would take me on a journey to get back home; an often brutal journey at times, but one with amazing results. Unfortunately I said no. I chose again to live life as if I was in control and responsible for all that needed to be done. I chose to live as if I still had no hope.

So for 16 years, even though I had hope and a way back home to the garden via the Cross; I chose to wander the wasteland again in self-effort, self-will and self-determination. The path of re-entry to the garden was right there in front of me; a path of sanctification that would completely change the landscape of my soul from a wasteland to a garden. I saw the light, received it in my spirit, and then turned around and walked right back into the wasteland. Why?

I believe it was because although I was given hope through what Jesus did on the cross, I never took possession of it. It hadn't been realized in my soul. It wasn't firmly and securely anchored in me. I still believed my way was better. I could make it back home on my own using God as an occasional helper when I would get stuck or be in a jam. Otherwise, "I got this!" No, I didn't.

Again for the next 16 years I grinded out my life of self-determination.

During this timeframe, I read about 500 books in addition to reading the Bible every day. I went to church and volunteered in some capacity to serve every Sunday. I mentored young Christians and lead a plethora of non-believers to salvation. I myself was tutored by over a dozen mentors. I had over 75 pastors as clients and every one of them would pour some bit of knowledge into me. My life and schedule represented someone who was rocking it for the Kingdom of God. But inside I was dying; I was exhausted and had completely lost all of my joy. Life was one big grind! My decision to go back to the wasteland after salvation and try to work life out on my own to please God had run out of fuel; I was done! I needed a way out of the wasteland again.

RESTORATION BEGINS

Three days after I experienced my brokenness, I attended a weekend Christian conference in Atlanta. I had no idea what to expect or why I was even going. All I knew is that I needed help. I needed hope from my desperate situation or I was going to die. But when I arrived at the conference I had the greatest revelation of my Christian life, I was already dead! Galatians 2:20 would now become the verse that would begin the restoration process in my soul: ("I have been crucified with Christ and I no longer live, but Christ lives in me."). After the conference I began to experience my restoration. I started to meet with a counselor once a week for the next year. It was a long and arduous process, but it had its purpose. And that purpose was Christ himself! I learned that our soul is comprised of our will, our mind and our emotions. During my counseling I was able to experience God beginning to conform my broken will to His, renewing my mind and balancing my emotions. All of a sudden I realized that I was a living example of Psalm 23. He, the Lord, was restoring my soul!

About midway through the year as I was vacationing at the beach with some friends when I was awakened in the middle of the night from what I thought was a nightmare. But as I began to talk with God that morning, He opened my eyes to what I really saw. My dream was a vision of myself leaving an island and crossing a bridge to my new destination. What I remember was that the island represented my old life, the self-life! I had been trapped on that island for forty-five years. On that island were death and all its ugly trappings, enticements and distortions of that which is good. It just reeked of the self-life! I began to see myself walking across a bridge headed to a new place. I could tell this place was accepting and that it had bright light, a sense of peace, warmth and most of all it had life! Even though I realized that I was leaving my old, decaying self-life behind, I could not help but feel a sense of grieving. That old man was the only me I ever knew. Though I had been saved, and living as a professed Christian for fifteen years, I was still operating out of my own self-will. I was still performing morally to gain God's acceptance. I still had to be in control, but now I was in control for all the so called right reasons. I was going to be a warrior for God, but in my own strength, even if it killed me. And it almost did!

So now, I began to understand God's purpose in brokenness. You see, brokenness is the bridge from 'us to Him'. **Walking across the bridge of brokenness is learning to be in unison, or one, with God!** It is our spirit experiencing life with His spirit. There is no longer separation with God. Christ is my life and mine is His. Brokenness is the bridge that brings our life together with His! That unity is what I have always desired, "…Never will I leave you, never will I forsake you!" (Hebrews 13:5) Even though I didn't realize it at that time I was never alone on the island of self, and I know now that I'll never be alone again. And although the bridge of brokenness is the initial, ultimate, and often times the most painful bridge to cross it takes us from the self-life (the wasteland) to life in Christ (the garden). There are many other bridges to cross along the journey to better experience the freedom that comes with living in a state of brokenness and surrender to God's perfect will!

MORE BRIDGES TO CROSS

I believe that once we begin to cross the bridge of brokenness leading from self-life to Christ's life, we inevitably enter into the 'rest' of God (Hebrews 4:11). Entering God's rest is a state of being; God is in the driver's seat and we are in the passenger seat enjoying the ride. As we rest in God we encounter many other bridges that need to be crossed. And though they all may not be as daunting as the bridge of brokenness, they are all important to complete the journey. Some will be scarier than others. Some will be harder to cross. Some will have unforeseen challenges. Some will be obvious and others will surprise. And, some may even be crossed simultaneously. But, no matter the size, length or degree of difficulty, they all are necessary as we make our way back home.

Detour to Destiny

There is the bridge from 'detour to destiny'; where we leave behind our plan and agenda for our lives and begin to seek out and surrender to God's plan for us. Our detours from God's perfect plan for our life becomes shorter because we now have the greatest GPS system in the world, the Holy Spirit. We become free from our own mistakes that take us on many lengthy detours leading to frustration, confusion and pain. Our forty year wanderings can now be eleven day journeys, just as God intended for the Israelites, as He leads us into our Promised Land!

Bondage of Lies to the Mind of Christ

There is the bridge that leads from 'the bondage of lies to the mind of Christ'. Here is where God renews our mind and replaces all the lies we have believed with truth. He teaches us to take captive every thought and relate them to His Word (II Corinthians 10:4-5). In this place we learn to no longer conform to the patterns of this world (Romans12:2). We move from lie based thinking to understanding our identity in Christ and the truth of who we really are. Knowing who we are in Christ is the freedom that Christ himself promises to everyone who accepts the truth. And the truth is this, He came to rescue us from death so we can live with him forever. (John 8:36)

Judgment to Acceptance

There is the bridge that leads from 'judgment to acceptance', that confirms our new identify and the proper source of good works. This bridge transfers us from 'performance based acceptance' to 'acceptance based performance'. When we realize that we are totally accepted by God because of our identity in Christ, who is now our righteousness, we are then free to perform out of love and gratitude rather than fear. We no longer fear the wrath of God for our mistakes and imperfections. We are free to be ourselves. (Romans 8:1). This is where we leave behind the perfectionist in us and learn to rely on the Perfect One who lives in us instead. I've struggled with being judgmental all my life and I have a feeling I will need to cross this bridge many times in my journey.

<u>Condemnation to Freedom</u>

There is the bridge that leads from 'condemnation to freedom'. Here we leave the Old Testament law and enter the New Testament age of grace! It is here that we discover that people are the priority with God, not religious codes of behavior! We are now free to love people despite their imperfections, where we once rejected them because of imperfections. As a recovering perfectionist I need to cross this bridge and never look back. I am sick and tired of rejecting people in my life because they aren't perfect! News flash: Breaking alert! Neither am I! Not only has God not rejected me, but has accepted me just the way I am and that is exactly what He expects from me. Crossing this bridge gives me the freedom to love others just as they are. As a matter of fact that is exactly why Jesus gave His life for us; (Galatians 5:1), "It is for freedom that Christ has set us free." And freedom to me is the ability to live and love as Christ does!

<u>Lust to Love</u>

There is the bridge that leads from 'lust to love'. It is here we begin to leave the event driven life of control and enter the land of relationships. We cease to see others as an object that exists only to satisfy our wants and pleasures; that is lust! We stop using people to get our needs met because Christ is our life and fills us with everything we need to experience true joy. (Philippians 4:19) We also learn that people are no longer obstacles that impede life, but are opportunities with whom to share life. Here, we simply get to enjoy relationships and leave the rest to God! Crossing this bridge helps us to understand that people are not always events that have to end. Rather, they can and should develop into relationships that last forever. God centered relationships are filled with love; and Love always perseveres! (1ˢᵗ Corinthians 13)

This is just the beginning and these are just a few of the bridges that we will cross in our journey with God. But I have also found that crossing these bridges will change the landscape of our life. Our lives will change from 'desolate wastelands' to 'gardens and vineyards' (Ezekiel 36:35). In our self-life there is a distinct odor and it is called 'flesh'. Some might even call it the 'stench of death', whatever you prefer! But it reeks and the more it is fueled by the desires of our flesh the worse it gets. If our will remains unbroken after salvation, our soul will continue to exist in the wasteland trying to obtain life through our own efforts. But we were made for more. We were made for better. We were made to be sanctified, set apart, and transformed into His Image.

To remain in the wasteland after being set free from death by Jesus is like winning the lottery and never cashing in the ticket! It would be a shame to miss out on all the benefits of the cross and the joys of life in the garden. There is no true life in the desolate wasteland of self. But for those destined for Christ as their life, there is hope! (Romans 8:30) Life in Christ is like living in a garden, and God is our constant tender! He continually pulls the weeds (lies) from our heart and replaces them with flowers (truth). And that's where God is taking us, to a garden deep down in our hearts, where we are surrounded by the fragrances and fruit of life. Such as love, joy, peace, patience, kindness, goodness, faithfulness, gentleness and self-control! This was our life experience before the Fall. It was life the way God originally intended it to be. It is a life we can once again reclaim by accepting his offer to rescue us and be at peace with Him.

THE FRONT LINE IN THE SPRITUAL WAR

Many times in my Christian life I have uttered this prayer; "God, I want to be a warrior in your Kingdom. I want to be on your 'special ops' team. I want to be on the front line of this war with evil! Please make me that man!" Now I know this prayer sounds like a noble prayer, one that might even get me a lead role in a movie like 'Braveheart' or 'Gladiator'. But what I failed to realize is that both leading men in those movies died! And in my ignorance I had no idea that to become a 'special ops warrior' on the front lines of the war between God and Satan's evil force, I would have to die! I've been told, "Be careful what you pray for because you just might get it!" I just could never have imagined this prayer being answered in the way that it was.

The principle at work here is this: 'the way up in God's Kingdom is down'! In order to be promoted you must be broken, and to reign you must die! And death it was! That is why I experienced the brokenness which eventually led to the death of my self-life. I was having my prayer answered and receiving the desires of my heart. I was being promoted to the front line! It just felt backwards and upside down. It was unnatural for my flesh to understand how the Kingdom of God works. Everything with God is opposite from the world. That is why God tells us not to love the world (1st John 2:15-17). The world is deceiving and its path is one that leads to death. The world tells us that living and experiencing true life is possible without God. The world tells us that we can do it on our own, make it on our own and survive on our own. It tells us we can be what we want and do what we want all apart from God and still survive. But that's just it; survive not thrive!

Fighting on the front lines is about resting. It is about thriving and living life in an abundant way. For those who are in Christ, we can come to the conclusion that operating in the flesh (self-willed, self-determined life) is an exhausting process which eventually destroys every area of life. The good news is that God can take our ruins and rebuild our lives through brokenness. And when He does, Christ as our life will begin to restore all that we have lost. His restoration causes us to lie down in green pastures like trees planted near streams of water. When you've entered that rest you are able to hand the reigns of life over to God and watch as He directs your life to the best possible one you can have. That is the mystery of brokenness. When you're broken you are finally ready to fight on the front line, but that's when you realize its God doing the fighting for you!

I could never have imagined that fighting on the front line and resting would be so intricately connected. What I've learned is when we work God rests, and when we rest God works! God wants to do for us. He loves us! His way is always better! He knows we can't fight the giants in our life on our own. David needed to invoke the Spirit of God to defeat Goliath. (1st Samuel 17:45) "David said to the Philistine, "You come against me with sword and spear and javelin, but I come against you in the name of the Lord Almighty…'" David ended up slaying the nine foot tall giant Goliath because he had God fighting for him. David was a rutty little red headed boy probably half Goliath's height and a fraction of his weight. David was at rest in his relationship with God and was so confident in his God to have His back that all he needed to do was call on the name of God, rest and victory was assured. David had learned how to fight on the front line.

I was not prepared to discover the type of people I would find on the front line. The people there are at rest. They are not the proud. They are not self-reliant. These frontline soldiers are surrendered! They have surrendered their hearts to God. They are the broken. They are the meek, the humble and the peacemakers. They are seated at the right hand of the father, joint heirs with Christ. They have no life of their own but the life of Christ in them because of the cross. They have crossed the bridge from 'doing for self' to 'being in Christ'. They are the true children at rest and fighting soldiers of God!

Thank you God (Romans 8:15) for the indescribable gift of brokenness! **I now know that 'Brokenness is the Bridge' and the bridge is Christ Himself!** I cannot wait to see what next year brings; I know the journey has just begun!

OUT OF THE WASTELAND
Year Two

Last year I began a journey from my self-willed, self-determined life to total dependence on God. Or shall we say from the wasteland to a garden. It is a journey I've come to discover that every disciple of Christ must travel without exception: it is a journey of brokenness. There are no short cuts, loopholes or ways to speed up the process. It is all in God's hands and in His time. Brokenness is the rite of passage into a life of usefulness to God. Without brokenness one will be at best a hindrance to the work of God in their life. Although brokenness may be extremely painful at times, it is a gift from God. It sets us free from the prison of self and allows us the freedom to find and walk that narrow path that few will ever find (Matthew 7:14). And that path will always lead us to a garden better known as 'God's Rest'. Our lives are like gardens and God is our one and only constant gardener. It is His responsibility and His alone to restore and maintain the garden. God is the only one capable to turn our lives from desolate wastelands into flourishing gardens. The type of life we live comes from the condition of our hearts. That is why Gods word says, "Above all else, guard your heart, for everything you do flows from it" (Proverbs 4:23). A heart at rest will lead to a life at rest and will produce much fruit. And that is where I found myself at the conclusion of 2011, beginning to experience God's rest, a place unknown to me before I experienced brokenness. I have spent the last year watching God begin to restore and rebuild my heart, a process that can be quite painful. It requires diligence on the part of the gardener God, coupled with patience and trust on our part. I found it fascinating as I watched and experienced God begin the restoration process of my heart and life. I want to share with you what the eyes of my heart were able to witness as I walked with God on the next part of my journey.

THE DESOLATE WASTELAND

Before we embark on our journey we need to understand the condition of an unbroken life, or life before brokenness. The Bible refers to it as 'a desolate wasteland'. Interestingly, this is the picture of life after the Fall when Adam and Eve were tempted by Satan, willingly disobeyed God and cast out of the Garden of Eden, our original paradise home. As a consequence they were condemned to live in an unstable world fraught with conflict, disease and decay. Unlike Eden, in the wasteland one is born into a life that is marked with physical and spiritual death. Ironically, it is also a land with glimpses of what was and what could be to remind us of our longing to go back home. In this land, we reside but are lost; we suffer but have no relief; we are doomed yet destined for worse. The Bible paints a very gloomy picture of the wasteland, which exists both in the physical world and in our hearts and minds. Throughout history, we have tried every human way possible to escape the wasteland but to no avail. You see, our crime was too great, the penalty too high to be recompensed and thus we find ourselves prisoners powerless to remedy the situation. Existentially and intuitively we all know this to be the case. We live in a world, and experience life, in need of repair but we can't fix it on our own. What we need is to be set free and restored by a power greater than ourselves. We need divine intervention.

Typically when we find mention of a wasteland in the bible it is associated with the picture of an abandoned and overgrown land. A desert so dry and void of water that is no longer capable of producing a crop. Its source of water, the river, has ceased flowing into it. It is described as containing thorns, thistles, and briers. Weeds have completely replaced all the fruit bearing plants and flowers. Life in the wasteland is exhausting because all work done here is in our own effort (flesh or self-will) and produces very little fruit if any at all. We know the flesh is an exhaustible resource with a short shelf life and is only good for producing trials! Work done in the flesh is counterproductive to works produced by the spirit (Galatians 5:17). Understand that before one is broken almost everything that believer tries to do for God is an act of the flesh, an attempt to find life apart from Him and most assuredly a hindrance to His purpose for their life.

So what is the cause of this desolation? I believe that it is a heart condition caused by pride. As said earlier, what is in one's heart will manifest in their life. In the book of Jeremiah, chapter 17 verse 9 reads," The heart is deceitful above all things and beyond cure. Who can understand it?" After looking deeper into this verse in an attempt to learn more about it, I came across an interesting Hebrew interpretation which translates "Covered with bloody footprints and makes it become chaotic". And from that I began to get a picture of what a life looks like when the heart has been trampled by the heels of our Enemy (Satan) and left in ruins. When we think our way is better (pride) and attempt to find life outside of God and His authority, we remove ourselves from His protection. This removal is best described in Isaiah 5:2,"Now I am going to tell you what I am going to do to my vineyard: I will take away its hedge, and it will be destroyed: I will break down its wall and it will be trampled. I will make it a wasteland, neither pruned nor cultivated, and briers and thorns will grow there. I will command the clouds not to rain on it". When we choose to do life apart from God is when the Enemy (Satan) gains access to our hearts and walks all over it leaving behind his bloody footprints along with a sense of chaos and despair!

Since we now have an understanding of the desolate wasteland, let us look deeper into its content. We know it is full of briers, thistles and thorns, which are all weeds and represent lies from the Enemy and this world. They can range from lies about our identity in Christ, His finished work on the cross and the character of God. They can also be very personal lies about our looks, self-worth or our own character. Whatever the lie is the enemy will use it to try and condemn us. His purpose in condemning us is to drive us to the law. The law attracts the flesh and will tell us that we have to 'do' more things in order to be accepted by God. Such as read our bible more, pray more, serve more at church, confess our sins, every one of them every day, give more money and take a mission trip to a foreign land. And by doing all these things in an increasing manner we maybe, just maybe will become acceptable to God. These are all commendable when done with the right motive, but the enemy knows all these things when done in our own efforts will just lead to spiritual pride and eventually exhaustion. But it is what comes natural to the one operating in the flesh.

Since Adam first sinned we all have within us our sin nature that operates in the flesh, our self-will! And though we may pray..."Father not my will, but your will be done"...it is only lip service until brokenness occurs. In this wasteland an unbroken life will strive harder and harder to find life by imposing its will over and over again. It will manipulate every circumstance and situation it can in order to maintain control of life. But those existing in this wasteland have poor eye sight and fail to see the lie (weed) that the Enemy has introduced to them. It is the 'illusion of control'. Because of the lack of water and nutrients (Gods word and spirit) in the wasteland, those existing in it fail to understand that what they perceive as control is really an illusion! We are never in control, God is! The Enemy wants us to think we are in control in order to convince us to never let go of our life that it may be saved (Mathew 16:25). So we hold on to our life and our will with everything we have. If held onto tight enough and long enough with still no sign of life, we will eventually become desperate and begin demanding our rights!

Ah yes....our right to live as we choose apart from God! The secret weapon used to push those in the wasteland further into chaos and despair. Self-determination or what some consider our "personal rights" is the largest of all the weeds in the wasteland. The huge problem with such rights is that they are not really rights at all. They are lies that have been told to us in order to make us feel as if God owes us something. And once the wasteland is completely full with rights of self-determination, it becomes the land of entitlement.

Ah yes...entitlement! The core belief that somehow we deserve what we believe to be best for our lives and the lives of others. It is the key that locks the door to the wasteland. Once entitlement enters the wasteland there is very little chance one can escape its snare. Entitlements can become so deceptive and produce so much false hope that the one entangled in them may find it impossible to live without. In fact, they would be willing to do just about anything to keep them. Those imprisoned by entitlement have become its slaves. After all, it is what they set out after, a life free from the restrictions of God and His authority; a life of self-determination! They can now roam about the wasteland carrying their right to rule themselves and the entitlements that come with it, but they will do so as prisoners and slaves to their own desires. They can go anywhere they want and do whatever they want, but they can never leave the wasteland. They have attained their autonomy from God.

And that is why brokenness, no matter how painful or frightening, is a gift from God. Brokenness is the bridge that helps us to throw off every hindrance and entanglement (Hebrews chapter 12: verse 1) that has ensnared us in the wasteland and frees us to walk through the valley to enter the door of hope and encounter the new landscapes that ultimately leads us back home.

THE PRISON OF SELF

I spent the first 45 years of my life in a prison of self, trying to manufacture a sense of self-worth and meaning. Before I became a Christian at the age of 29 I was like King Solomon in his youth; "I denied myself nothing my eyes desired; I refused my heart no pleasure. (Ecclesiastes chapter 2)" I tried just about everything to find peace and happiness only to realize that chasing after life's pleasures was foolish and meaningless. Once I was converted, I focused on the pursuit of wisdom and financial success; this too was meaningless and resulted in self-righteousness. All of these pursuits lead me to ask myself a question; what is wrong with me? That is a hard question to ask, especially as one who claimed to experience spiritual rebirth years ago only to find himself sitting alone in the prison of self. But in reality, that is where I had been ever since I could remember. I now know why I have felt so defective and alone all my life; I was deceived! Somehow the Enemy convinced me at an early age that God could not be fully trusted. So even though I handed over to Him my eternal destiny I really didn't trust God with my temporal present and future. If life was going to happen, I would have to be the one to make it happen. That's the lie that leads to the prison of self and life in the wasteland and I bought it hook, line and sinker.

Living in a prison of self in the far back corner of the wasteland is a lonely existence. It doesn't matter if you are in a room full of people, you are still alone. As a matter of fact, the larger the crowd the lonelier you feel. Unfortunately this is a place many people go to escape reality. Facing life's challenges and struggles can be extremely fearful to someone who doesn't experience love and trust. Worst of all fear leads to isolation; a place where God knows is extremely dangerous for us. Isolation is where our Enemy does his greatest work. He begins to whisper in our ears which at this point are deaf toward God and begins to impute lies into our thinking. These lies damage our self-esteem and self-worth as they attack our identity and condemn our very existence. Once established they produce wrong thinking and a myriad of spiritual, physical and emotional ailments. If the Enemy can convince us that God cannot be fully trusted, it will propel us into a life of self-effort and separate us from the true source of love; God himself! I know, I suffered greatly from this way of living.

A WAY OUT

I believe there is a point in which the human soul can no longer take the isolation and pain of the wasteland. There just comes a time when enough is enough. The life governed by self-effort no longer delivers on its promise and we need a way out. So after 45 years in the wasteland, 29 as a non-Christian and 16 as a Christian, I could hear God's soft quiet voice calling to me as I sat in my prison of self in the farthest corner of the wasteland. I looked up and answered that call with a prayer from Psalm 142 verses 6-7, "Listen to my cry, for I am in desperate need; rescue me from those who pursue me, for they are too strong for me. Set me free from my prison, that I may praise your name." From desperation comes deliverance and I was desperate! The pain of remaining in the wasteland was starting to give way to the possibility of a better land.

That soft quiet voice I heard calling my name began to allure me out of my prison of self. But to my surprise, this alluring came in a totally unexpected way. You see, I was immediately drawn deep down into a valley hand crafted by God and unique for every single person seeking to escape the wasteland. I knew it would be a brutal and excruciating journey through the valley, but one with a great outcome. So buckle up and join me; it's going to be a rollercoaster ride!

ENTERING THE REST

I believe that for my entire life I have been on a quest for **peace**: my personal 'vision quest'. In the Native American culture, a vision quest is a rite of passage through which a child becomes an adult. It is a turning point in one's life intended to help them find their true identity and purpose in life. A vision quest requires one to spend much time in seclusion which provides time for deep communion with God. So when I first was broken back in January of 2010, it was as if I entered into 'chrysalis', the stage when a caterpillar enters a cocoon before becoming the perfect butterfly; definition, 'A protected stage of development'. God has a very distinct purpose when He places one of His children into chrysalis and that is to produce a mature adult (Ephesians 4:14-15). The caution here, do not emerge from chrysalis before God's appointed time of transition. Emerging prematurely from one's chrysalis is very dangerous. It will cause you to emerge underdeveloped, unprepared and weak like an infant or child. Wanting to break free from this cocoon like stage was something I struggled with for the two and a half years preceding my brokenness in January 2010.

God's purpose in transforming us from children to mature adults is to change our nature from being childish to being childlike! Acting childish involves throwing tantrums, pity parties, tattle telling, demanding your rights, having your own way and never admitting you are wrong! Those are the characteristics of a child enslaved in the wasteland. But to be at rest, listening, learning, obeying, trusting and experiencing joy, is to be childlike and are the characteristics of a mature adult at rest. Maturity is God's purpose for every believer on this planet! And after 18 years as a believer I could finally see the transformation from child to childlike adult taking place in my life. My quest for peace was about to go to the next stage and it required maturity! And let me tell you, maturity can only be produced by persevering all the way to the journey's end.

LESSON #1

Learning to hear God's voice above all others is lesson #1! The Holy Spirit made the verse John 10:27 the cornerstone to this lesson; "My sheep listen to my voice; I know them, and they follow me". The Holy Spirit also reminded me that besides being able to hear God's voice, I was not to listen to strange voices! Being able to distinguish between the voice of God and the voices of strangers was going to be imperative to obeying God and following Him. It was also going to require a tremendous amount of time just sitting with God and listening. I call it, 'time on the porch with Papa!' This time alone with God led me to ask myself a tough twofold question; "Who has authority from God to speak into my life? And who has an opinion that matters to me?"

The picture that came to mind after asking that question was that of my life before brokenness when I was in the wasteland. I saw the garden of my life trampled with bloody footprints and lying in ruins because I had no boundaries. The walls and boundaries of God's protection were nonexistent in my life. Unhealthy people don't have boundaries and therefore are susceptible to the influence of strange voices. Anyone can speak into their life, whether it is a curse or a blessing, because they have no defense against the strange voices. There is no gate keeper to keep the voice out because there are no walls to attach a gate to. There is neither a watchman in the watchtower to spot the strange voice before it enters because the watchtower has been abandoned as well. That is life in the wasteland! A defenseless life open to anyone and anything the Enemy throws at you.

But when you begin to distinguish and listen to the voice of God, you will hear His first promise of this journey. It is found in Isaiah 43:18-19, "Forget the former things; do not dwell on the past. See, I am doing a new thing! Now it springs up; do you not perceive it? I am making a way in the wilderness and streams in the wasteland!" This is the promise of **rest**oration I believe God gives to those who have come to the end of themselves (brokenness) and are now willing to exchange their life and their way of doings things for the Life that God has purposed for them. A life of resting in Him!

WE NEED TO TALK

The end of something inside of me happened in July of 2012. Not sure what was going on deep down in my heart, soul and spirit, but something wasn't quite right. I came home after a long day of work in the blistering heat of a mid-summer day in Atlanta feeling hopeless and empty and I had no idea why. But deep down inside my spirit I knew something was wrong and God was at the center of it. I walked in my house, dropped my work case on the floor in the foyer, walked to the living room, sat on my couch and as serious as I have ever been said to God, "we need to talk!" It wasn't time for prayer, I needed to have one of those let's get it out in the open, lay it all out on the table, listen to me carefully, I'm drowning in hopelessness and despair, please talk to me conversations with God. I was thinking I really needed God to throw me a rope but was afraid of what I might do with it. This was one of those times in life when you know that something has to change but you have absolutely no idea what it is. Do you know what I am talking about? People will come to this place in life and utter such phrases as, 'I know something is wrong but I just can't put my finger on it!' Or, 'I feel as if someone or something is trying to get my attention but I don't know what about!' It could be as simple as, 'Something's not right!' Or even better yet in Jersey terms, 'Dude???!!! What's going on?' Any way you say it there was an issue deep within me that needed to be dealt with. So talk we did.

I remember so clearly how the conversation went after my initial words of "we need to talk" because the silence in the room was deafening. God said, "Okay, go ahead." And I said back to Him, "I don't know what's wrong but I hate my life!" And then I proceeded to give God a few options as if I was the one in control and calling the shots. Here were my options," You have to deliver me from whatever this is or take me out of this world! I can't keep going on living the way I am or I will die!" I wasn't kidding. This was another end of the road point for me in my journey of brokenness. I had gone as far as I could go living the way I was living and if something did not change I truly felt as if I would not be able to continue living. Have you ever been there? If you have you know the sense of hopelessness and despair that can make it hard just to breathe. But that is where I was, trapped in despair and I needed to be rescued.

Here is some good news; God is in the business of rescuing those who are in desperate need. In His infinite wisdom He is able to wait patiently for us to come to the end of ourselves. Then when we are finished striving in our own strength He can begin to do what only God can do, lead us to the best life He has for us. I know that I am not alone in feeling this way. Many of God's servants have come to this place of despair and have cried out to God to be rescued. King David was one of them. He wrote many of the Psalms while he was despairing for his life. But it was Psalm 142 again that really helped me reach out to God at this time. I was lead back to verses 6 and 7 of that psalm and would pray them to God for a long time to come.

They read as so, "Listen to my cry for I am in desperate need; rescue me from those who pursue me, for they are too strong for me. Set me free from my prison that I may praise your name." That would be my prayer to carry me through this season. I needed God to listen to my cry for help because I was desperate to be set free from what felt like a prison inside of me.

Now I am pretty sure God wasn't answering my ultimatum when He began to give me His initial instructions of what was going to take place next in light of my cry for help. God is such a perfect Father. He let me vent and listened with compassion and then replied like a perfect father would. I somewhat already knew what His first response would be because God always wants us to choose life over death. And life it was! His first words to me were, "I am not taking you out of this world. I am not finished with you yet!" So once it was established that I would continue my journey in this world God began to set some changes in motion and the first one was quite radical.

Now I am not stating here that what happened next will happen to everyone who is in this kind of situation. It was what I believe God felt was best for me and necessary to equip me for the journey ahead. Here is what God said to me next, "The first thing I want you to do is give me your tongue!" It sounded a bit strange to me at first but deep down inside I knew exactly what God was referring to. He was going to give me the gift of speaking and praying in tongues. And that is what I heard next, "I will give you the gift of tongues." God went on to clarify to me why He was doing this. It was because I was a type 'A' whose life's motto was 'If it is going to get done I will have to do it myself!' And that was a huge part of my problem. I was trying to do this life all by myself. I have always chosen to do this life on my own. It was what gave me a false sense of control and security. But it is an illusion the Enemy sells us to make us think we are in control and therefore usurp God's authority in our life.

One thing I knew. God did not want me to control or interfere with His plan to rescue me from this pain. It was to be the Holy Spirit interceding on my behalf with perfect prayers that would lead me to God's best. Paul writes of this in the book of Romans 8:26, "In the same way, the spirit helps us in our weakness. We do not know what we ought to pray for, but the Spirit himself intercedes for us through wordless groans. And he who searches our hearts knows the mind of the Spirit, because the Spirit intercedes for

God's people in accordance with the will of God." So I was about to get the best help possible to lead me out of this mess; the Holy Spirit praying perfect prayers on my behalf!

So as I sat there in amazement of what I just experienced, the second thing I needed to do was made clear to me. God's next instruction was, "Then put your house up for sale!" This did not shock me as much as the first command. I had already been contemplating selling my house. It was just too big for me to live in by myself. It was becoming a burden. The walls began to cave in on me and every day I stayed there I felt more and more trapped. So I knew my next phone call would be to find a real estate agent and get my house on the market. I was fine with that. Actually, I felt a little bit relieved knowing this burden of a house would soon be lifted off my shoulders and the wheels of God's plan to change my life would now be in motion!

But the third instruction that I heard from God was the most nerve wracking part of the whole conversation. It was this, "And then hold on to your suspenders because everything in your life is going to look like it is falling apart, but do not worry! I am just going to be rearranging everything to the way it should be. I am going to lead you to your best life possible!" And fall apart it did!

Within six months of that prayer I went from living in a five bedroom house to living in the basement of a friend's house. I had one of my two companies shut down which reduced my income by eighty percent. I entered a battle to receive monies owed to me, about a third of my life's savings. I have to admit, there were times I sat in that basement and said to myself, "What was I thinking praying that prayer!" But in reality I knew it was going to be a season, a really tough one, but one I needed to go through to get to where my heart desired to be, that is, where God wanted me to be.

LETTING GO AND HOLDING ON

Now that God and I had our talk and are on the same page going forward, I want to explain a fundamental change that has to occur if we are to hear God's voice and walk with him. Let go of God's hand and let Him take hold of yours! Why is this so important? Because until brokenness occurs we will tend to take hold of God's hand in an attempt to pull Him in the direction we feel is best for our lives. It is how we find ourselves in most of the predicaments we get into. Our attempt to lead God to our best is an act of the flesh and will always produce trials. But when we let go of God's hand and surrender our right to do life our own way, God can then begin to lead us by His Spirit to the life He has for us. Rick Warren calls it the "Purpose Driven Life!" It is the life of a mature believer and is purposed by God for his Glory and our good. Our responsibility in this life is to listen to God's voice, obey Him immediately and let Him lead us by His holy hand for the purposes He has set before us.

Personally, I found this exchange left me both anxious and excited at the same time. This new way of walking through life was completely contradictory to the way I was accustomed. I never realized just how much I walked in the flesh, how much I desired to be in control of my life and lead the way or how much I expected God to bless my plans and efforts! So as I let go of God's hand and let Him take hold of mine He immediately began to speak to me and the first thing we talked about was surrendering certain rights that I was holding on to dearly. Letting go and surrendering rights can leave you extremely anxious and fearful. After all, it's likely we have held onto them our entire life. But remember, these so called rights are actually lies of the Enemy used to enslave us with fear. And what is fear? **False Evidence Appearing Real!** Being enslaved to your rights and entitlements is a false fear. It only exists in our mind and in our misinformed beliefs. It's wasteland thinking! So in order to change our life we must change our mind, that is, repent. We must change from our way of thinking to God's way of thinking! This renewing of the mind begins with the surrendering of our rights, which appears to be frightening but is actually liberating. It's the road to freedom.

So the first rights God asked me to give up were my rights to know and understand why! Though there were many rights to be surrendered these were the two most stubborn and enslaving rights that needed to go. Now there are legitimate reasons and times to ask why and to know what for. They may even save your life if there is a dangerous request asked of you. But what I am talking about here is stubbornness; the inability to allow someone who is older, wiser, more mature and with your best interest at heart to lead you.

God was able to help me surrender these rights by bringing me back to my childhood and showing me the roots of these so called rights. God asked me one day what made me the angriest when I was a child? It took about two seconds before the Holy Spirit brought to my mind the answer; when my mom used the phrase "because I said so!" That would ignite my fury for sure. I was not going to do anything for anyone unless I was told why and understood its purpose! I had a right to know and understand why and I demanded it be met! Well, God made it abundantly clear that the right to ask and understand why, or put another way, the right to be stubborn, could not be a part of my walking by faith. If I was going to let go of His hand and let Him take hold of mine and lead me to His purpose for my life, the right to be stubborn would have to go! I would have to learn to walk by faith and not by sight (2nd Corinthians 5:7/KJV)!

REVERSING THE FLOW

Then something else began to happen that was frightening to begin with but ultimately turned out to be one of the coolest experiences of this year. As soon as I had surrendered the 'right' to be stubborn, my spirit came to a halt. I had no idea what was happening but a sense of rest and relaxation began to come over me. It was as if the RPM's of my life and the noise they made had subsided and slowed to idle. I began to breathe easier and was able to hear with greater clarity. I was able to better distinguish the voice of God without all the distractions of my efforts to find life on my own. I guess you could say it was the first time in my life where I actually "stopped to take a look around and smell the roses!" Of course it was God who was the one to bring me to the complete stop, something I was unable to do on my own. Never the less, it was a place my heart had longed for all of my life!

Then, as soon as I had gotten comfortable with this new position of rest, it started to happen; the flow of my life began to reverse! With God holding my hand my body and spirit began to gently turn and face the opposite direction; toward God and not away from Him. It was as if I started moving back in the direction I had been striving from all my life. At first I felt out of control and was scared, but then I realized God had a hold of my hand and wasn't letting go. It also occurred to me that I was moving without any effort. It was an effortless flow that required one thing of me, rest! I was to sit in the passenger seat and enjoy the view of the journey ahead. There was no need for me to grab the steering wheel, or step on either the gas or the brake petal because there is a new driver in my life who's in total control and knows where we were going and how quickly we will get there. And though I have no idea where I am headed, how long it will take, or what obstacles lay ahead, I'm cool with it because my new driver does! I know at times I will be tempted to reach out with my hands to grab the wheel and steer or reach out with my foot to control the speed, but that's because I'm still human. But the farther down the road of this journey I go, the stronger my faith will grow and the deeper my trust will be in order to stay in a position of rest.

Here is an illustration God gave me to better understand 'Reversing the Flow'. It is like the life of a salmon. Yes, we're not salmon but follow me on this – you'll get the point. They are born and raised to become adult salmon which eventually will reproduce and keep the circle of life going. As a newborn they learn how to act as a salmon by imitating other salmon and following their natural instincts. Once they have developed and reached the stage of adulthood, they will feel the drive to reproduce and begin their quest for it. And like all other salmon they start off swimming together till they eventually find the river that will take them to their destination. Once they get to the river they realize that their destination is upstream. So with all the energy and strength they can muster they begin the challenge of swimming against the current for the rest of their life. But not only is this an exhausting process, it is a deadly one as well. Let's say you are one of the lucky salmon who doesn't get eaten by a bear lurking on the shores upstream and eventually makes it to the spawning grounds to reproduce. Although you think you have won by reaching your destination and getting to spawn, you ultimately die of exhaustion! And to me, death by exhaustion isn't winning! But for those salmon that realize the futility of this quest and stop swimming against the current in their own effort and allow the current to turn them around (reverse the flow), a new life awaits them downstream. A life of rest! Their journey will now seem effortless but will require trust! Although this new direction of going with the current is effortless and relaxing, it is also filled with persecutions. The other salmon won't like the fact that you have given up the struggle and the pursuit of happiness in your own effort. They will scream at you as you pass each and every one of them. They will say things like what are you doing? Who do you think you are? Do you think you are better than us? What's your plan? You're going the wrong way! That's not the way we do it! But don't listen to those strange voices and their persecutions (Mark 10: 29-30). You listen to the one voice (God) that counts and you let the current (Holy Spirit) simply guide you with ease down the river to a vast ocean of God's grace in which you can enjoy the 'rest' of your life!

Over all, what does reversing the flow mean? It is the active part of the journey that takes you from the law (our own effort) to grace (what Jesus has already done)! It is no longer grieving the Holy Spirit by going against His leading with self-will and disobedience. In Jersey terms reversing the flow is called, "Bang a U-EY!" You are going the wrong way and need to make a U-turn. Better yet, before you do so, change seats with God and let him grab the wheel. It is entering the rest of God and allowing the Holy Spirit to take hold of your hand and lead you on your life's journey. It is walking by faith!

RESPECT THE 'NO'

Here is the next lesson I was taught by God once the flow of my life had been reversed. Learn to say 'No', and respect the 'No' of God, others and yourself! So what is the significance of learning to say 'No'? It keeps you from one of the greatest traps of the wasteland, busyness! Our Enemy knows that if he can keep us busy doing things that are not from God he can almost render us useless for the kingdom of God. You see, we all grow up learning the difference between right and wrong, and if taught properly will be able to discern between good and bad choices. I would say most of us will succeed in learning to make good choices verses bad ones, with the exception of hardened criminals. Then possibly, some people will mature to the point of discerning between good and great choices and then choose the great. They are known as the movers and the shakers of this world, separating the exceptional from the average person. But what I am beginning to learn is that there is another level of decision making beyond the ability to choose between good and great. It is the ability to discern between the good, great and God! That is where the ability to say 'No' will take you; deeper into the garden where you can discern and hear God's voice calling you to choose and follow Him above all other choices in life, including the great ones! Until you are able to say 'No' to the bad, good and great choices in life you are not ready to choose and receive the God choices for your life. This is tough training, but it is 'training for reigning'. Those who want to reign in this life and the next must choose God above everything else. God's best is not a given in this life, you have to want it. And it only comes to those who through brokenness, have entered rest, learned to hear God's voice, allowed Him to take hold of their hand, reverse the flow of their life, say 'No' to worldly choices and follow Him. That's the process of maturing to adulthood. Mature adults not only know how to say 'No', they respect the 'No' of others and especially God by keeping healthy boundaries, and ultimately desiring nothing less than God's best for their life!

JUDGEMENT TO ACCEPTANCE – HERE WE GO AGAIN

I began to cross the bridge from judgment to acceptance last year but knew this bridge would require me to cross several times. Jesus said, "Do not judge, or you too will be judged. For in the same way you judge others, you will be judged, and with the same measure you use, it will be measured to you." (Matthew 7:1-2) So my introduction to this bridge came at the very end of last year (2011) while watching television. A headline rolled out on the screen indicating the latest minority owner of a major sports team. I immediately went into judgment mode and thoughts of fear and anxiety began to fill my mind. I started thinking such thoughts as, 'Here goes professional sports!', 'Nothing is sacred anymore… we are losing our nation and now the sports that we love..' And the thoughts went on and on for a few more minutes till I began to exhaust my mind with them. Then that still small quiet voice stepped in and said, 'We need to talk about this!' I knew right then as I felt it in my spirit that I was in for some brokenness and it would require crossing another bridge.

So God's first question to me was, 'Tell me what you know for sure about this person?' Though about twenty different judgments went through my mind, the only answer I could give God was, 'All I know is his name.' That's all I knew for sure, and the rest was pure judgment! God then posed a second question to me, 'Tell me what you felt in your heart when you were making judgments against this man because of his name?' The answer lit up in front of me like a neon sign, 'Fear!' That's what I felt, pure fear and all the anxiety and pain that comes with it. It's what I have been feeling all my life whenever I ate from the 'tree of the knowledge of good and evil.' You see that is why God never intended for Adam and Eve to eat from that tree, it would introduce judgment into the world along with all the fear and pain it brings. That's why Jesus said 'do not to judge'; because when we judge others all the pain that we attempt to inflict on them comes straight back to us. So now I realize the danger in judging others; the one doing the judging is the one who will suffer most! God's intention of breaking us from pronouncing judgment on others is to keep us from suffering its ill affects!

So where does the breaking of judgment in our lives lead us to; acceptance! It took me an entire year to realize where this bridge was leading me. It took several painful episodes in my life which I found myself experiencing the effects of judging others to open the eyes of my heart and see God's purpose in having me cross this bridge. God lead me to the book of Romans and began to open my eyes to the truth and the benefits of acceptance. Romans 14:13 says, "Therefore let us stop passing judgment on one another. Instead, make up your mind not to put any stumbling block or obstacle in your brother's way." We must choose to not judge others and it requires us to repent, change our mind to God's way of thinking about judgment. When the pain of judging others becomes too much to bare is when you have reached the crest of the bridge and can then begin your descent down the other side toward acceptance! So what are the benefits of acceptance? There are two that I have come to know. My pastor puts the first one like this, 'acceptance leads to influence!' Acceptance opens the door to influencing others towards God just as judging builds a wall that deters others away from God. And the second benefit is that it brings glory to God and not us! God's ultimate purpose in our lives is to bring glory to Him through us! Romans 15:7 says, "Accept one another, then, just as Christ accepted you, in order to bring praise to God." What a beautiful bridge!

TWO MORE BRIDGES TO CROSS

I encountered two more bridges this year. The first led from 'Hopelessness to Hope.' What is hopelessness? It is complete reliance on self apart from God. It is a fearful expectation of judgment and condemnation in our lives fueled by lies from our Enemy Satan. For the majority of my life I had lived with hopelessness. From my earliest years I believed the lie that life depended upon me and my ability to make things happen. I believed the lie that in order to be safe and successful I must control my surroundings. Therefore, the means always justified the end and I was supposed to do whatever it took to be in control. Usually this meant mastering the art of manipulation, which in turn drove me to become a perfectionist. The problem with perfectionists is that they don't qualify for relationships because they believe the lie that they don't have any needs and are self-sufficient, which then lands them in the prison of self, otherwise known as the wasteland! And that is one of the major characteristics of the wasteland, Hopelessness! So back in April of this year (2012) while walking with God I heard Him say to me that it was time for Him to restore my Hope. As I looked in front of us I saw a bridge and its name was 'Hopesteration'! Wow!!! I was staring at the bridge that would bring the restoration of hope in my life and deliver me from hopelessness. With God holding my hand we began to cross and He immediately started to transfer hope from me to Him. I began learning that hope in myself causes me to drain people and suck the life out of them (neediness), but hope in God will allow Him to impart life to others through me!

This is why it is so important to learn to hear the voice of God. Listening to God's voice will cause us to respond to others in love and bring us hope. Listening to strange voices causes us to react to others from our soul and drains the hope out of us and them. God's purpose in 'Hopesteration' is to restore and build healthy relationships in our lives. Our relationships in the wasteland tend to be filled with guilt and shame, two very powerful lies used by our enemy to condemn us and destroy all of our healthy relationships, while keeping us entangled in our unhealthy relationships. But when hope is transferred to the God of all hope, the lies (weeds) of guilt and shame are slowly removed by our gardener God allowing us to walk around the garden guiltless and shameless! All of the damaging effects of guilt and shame such as embarrassment, inferiority and loneliness begin to wither away as well. So as God and I crossed over the crest of this bridge and were walking down toward hope, my mind began to unravel why God had allowed me to experience so much suffering in my life. I think it is best described in Romans 5:1-5… "Therefore, since we have been justified through faith, we have peace with God through our Lord Jesus Christ, through whom we have gained access by faith into this grace in which we now stand. And we boast in the **hope** of the glory of God. Not only so, but we also glory in our sufferings, because we know that suffering produces perseverance; perseverance, character; and character **hope.** And **hope** does not put us to shame, because God's love has been poured out into our hearts through the Holy Spirit, who has been given to us." I now see suffering in a whole new light. Because God is for us not against us (Romans 8:13), He allows suffering to bring us hope and not to take our hope away. That's my God! And that's 'Hopesteration!' A life in the garden filled with hope as well as healthy, guiltless, shameless relationships!

A second bridge I encountered this year led me from 'planning to prayer'. I have a feeling I will be on this bridge for a very long time. The reason I believe this to be true is because this bridge has to do with taming the tongue (James 3:8). This part of the journey requires me to surrender my tongue and my desire to plan out my future. Very often I find myself on my knees before God explaining to Him my agenda and my plan to make it happen. All it would require from there is His blessing. But if I have learned anything from the journey of brokenness in life it is that I do not know what is best for me, only God does! That is the reason we need to go from planning to prayer. This however does not mean we do not plan at all. As I understand, we must place prayer before our plans. The book of Proverbs gives us much wisdom on this matter. In chapter 16 alone we find several verses to guide us across this bridge. In verse one it reads, "To man belong the plans of the heart, but from the Lord comes the reply of the tongue." This means that the final outcomes of the plans we make are in God's hands. This also requires a partnership between our efforts and God's control. God wants us seeking His guidance for the plans of our life, and then we can act with confidence as we trust Him to bring about the results. Verse three then reads, "Commit to the Lord whatever you do, and your plans will succeed." Here is where God teaches us about commitment and trust in the planning stages of life.

We must maintain a delicate balance: trusting God as if everything depended on Him, while working as if everything depended upon us. Commitment does not mean we become control freaks nor does it mean we are to be passive, it is about trust! And trust comes from a position of rest (Life in the garden). Joseph Prince defines rest as 'Holy Spirit directed activity'! Let that sink in for a while. Because it is a truth that will set us free from the frantic pace of pushing our agenda's in life ahead of God's plan for us. In a nutshell what this bridge has taught me is to be still before God and give careful thought to the words I will utter before Him, if any! I am learning that listening is the greatest form of prayer one can master. The one whose tongue has been tamed by the Lord will be the greatest listener of all. He will receive the Holy Spirit's guidance in making his plans and will show great patience and trust in living out God's plan for his life. Proverbs 16:6 says, "In his heart a man plans his course, but the Lord determines his steps." That is true partnership with God! And I believe that this partnership of trust is what it means to delight oneself in the Lord.

To delight in someone means to experience great pleasure and joy in his or her presence. And when we delight ourselves in the Lord is when we see the garden of our life truly begin to flourish and produce the abundance of life Jesus promised to give us here on earth and in eternity! Psalm 37:4…"Delight yourself in the Lord, and He will give you the desires of your heart." Prayer through listening leads us to God's plan for our life; it leads us to His best!

IN FULL BLOOM

To sum this all up, my quest for peace is in full bloom! My childhood dreams of peace are beginning to blossom before my very eyes! In my adult life I have been asked two particular questions with regularity; what was your childhood like? And what is the desire of your heart? When answering the first one a single word will always come to mind; chaos! My earliest memories as a little boy growing up in New Jersey are full of fear, anxiety and a total sense of chaos. I have often given those who have asked me to describe my childhood the same answer; "I feel as if I have been alone since I was 3 years old!" Why 3? I don't know. Maybe it is my way of saying I have never felt deeply loved, completely forgiven, fully pleasing or totally accepted by anyone, especially God! But thanks to Jesus Christ that lie has been uprooted in the Garden of my life so that the old way of thinking and living is gone; "Therefore, if anyone is in Christ, he is a new creation; the old is gone, and the new has come! (2ⁿᵈ Corinthians 5:17)

Wow!! That's what that verse means! Talk about a get out of jail free card; and that is exactly what brokenness is! Now, because of Jesus who is the living bridge of brokenness; I am deeply loved, completely forgiven, fully pleasing, totally accepted and absolutely complete in Christ. I love this journey to the Garden and know one thing for sure; I am never going back to the wasteland! I am on the 'Galatians 2:20 Bridge' with God leading the way and holding my hand; who would dare walk away from this journey! What is the desire of my heart? **Peace!!!** And that is exactly what Jesus promises to give; "Peace I leave with you; my peace I give you. I do not give to you as the world gives. Do not let your hearts be troubled and do not be afraid." I cannot wait to see what next year brings!

WALK TO REMEMBER
Year Three

In 2011 I discovered God's greatest gift to His children: Brokenness! It is a bridge that takes one from the self-life (the wasteland), to life in Christ (the garden). In 2012 I was taught many lessons and introduced to various other bridges that would be required to cross in order to complete this journey. After 45 years of exhaustion in the wasteland and a few years prepping for my journey to the Garden I heard that sweet soft voice of God say to me 'It's time to take a walk!' This wasn't a call to just stretch my legs but an invitation to live and learn what the righteous do best; 'They live by faith.' What is faith? Hebrews 11:1 tells us, "Now faith is confidence in what we hope for and assurance about what we do not see." This walk I was about to embark on would require a whole new level of faith and its purpose was to guide and lead me to the center of the garden. As I started walking I realized there would be more lessons that I needed to learn to prepare me for the journey. These lessons would open my eyes to many of the pitfalls and detours that had deceived me in the past. There were backward bridges, demonic gateways and forbidden doors that I had either crossed or opened which allowed the Enemy and his lies access to my mind. These passageways would need to be closed in order to begin my journey to the center of the garden. I had to learn two very important lessons from the onset, 'Never go back!' and 'Don't run ahead!' Only then could I truly understand that 'Walking in the garden with God is living in the moment!' It is not bringing up the past or predicting the future, it is now!

I now realize the first two years of my journey was a time of preparation. I was preparing to step out into the unknown with Jesus and experience the adventures that could lead to a life lived in the garden. I have read the

Bible almost every day for twenty years and have filled my mind with much scripture. But memorizing scripture and quoting the Bible are no longer working for me. It's time for me to get to know the author!

"WHAT IF" DISEASE

At the conclusion of last year, I realized that as a young boy I somehow accepted the lie that God could not be trusted with my future! I believe at the point of acceptance I contracted a disease; the 'What If' disease. In Linda Dillow's book, 'Calm my Anxious Heart', she writes about two spiritual 'IF' diseases; One being the 'If only' disease which looks to the past and grumbles about what God has given, or not given, to us and leads us to anger. Secondly she writes about the 'What If' disease, which looks to the future and worries about what God might allow and leads us to anxiety. Now, I have heard of people who have contracted 'Double Pneumonia', but I might be the first person to be diagnosed with 'Double What If!' That's how bad I suffered from the disease. I came to the point where I felt that if I didn't get healed from it I was going to die. But in order for anyone to receive spiritual healing, they must have peace and rest in their soul first. That's why brokenness is such a gift from God, it forces us to rest! Psalm 23:2 says it well, "He (the Lord) makes me lie down in green pastures (the garden)…" That's what brokenness does, it makes you rest! So I spent the first part of this year resting in Him preparing to walk away from this wasteland disease.

Now one of the most powerful side effects of the 'What If" disease is being paralyzed by fear; it is known as the 'paralysis of analysis!' This paralysis comes upon us when we are waiting for the 'what if's' of life to come to pass. Waiting for what might happen will cause the sturdiest of hearts to become anxious and begin employing control tactics to 'help God out'. Jeremiah 17: 5-6 tells us that those who trust in themselves (trust in man) and try to control every aspect of their life because of the fear of 'what if', turn their hearts away from the Lord and become like a bush in the desert and will not see prosperity when it comes. The 'What if" is a very debilitating disease that will drive us to believe that we are completely dependent on our own resources. That is what living in the wasteland is all about, being self-conscious, self-occupied and trusting in ourselves; it believes the lie that we are in control! The 'What if' disease with its deceptive powers can also lead one to a land that nobody wants to go! Let me tell you about it.

LAND OF ANXIETY

There is a place in the deep recesses of the Wasteland known as the 'Land of Anxiety'. It is a remote and desolate place where those who suffer from 'What if' will go and attempt to control their future by any means necessary. Those who have landed there are completely dependent on 'self' and consumed with worry. The 'Land of Anxiety' is a horrible place for two main reasons; first because it exists in our mind! In Matthew 6:34, Jesus says "Do not worry about tomorrow, for tomorrow will worry about itself…" A mind full of worry for the future steals your joy for today. Second, a mind full of worry cannot sense or appreciate the presence of God in the moment. That's why in year two I shared that learning to hear God's voice is the most important discipline to living the life God has for His children. It's always the first lesson taught on this journey because it teaches us to live in the moment (present) and not run out ahead of God. A wonderful quote that exemplifies this new way of thinking reads as follows;

"Neither go back in fear and misgiving to the past, nor in anxiety and forecasting to the future, but lie quiet under His hand, having no will but His" –H.E. Manning

Walking and living in the moment was first revealed to me in May this year when I felt led to read the 2nd Book of John. It speaks of the joy the apostle John found when seeing the children of God "walking in the truth", "walking in obedience" and finally "walking in love". Those are all ways of walking and living in the moment. I saw this as a description of those who walked with God in the Garden while living in the moment and experiencing His presence. To me these three types of walks represented walking in the fullness of God, in spirit, truth and love. My desire to live in the moment started to bloom in my heart! But then I came to verse 9 of 2nd John which reads; "Anyone who runs ahead and does not continue in the teaching of Christ does not have God..." Bam!!! It hit me right between the eyes! That was me. I was the one running out ahead of God! And that's when I also realized I had been living in the 'Land of Anxiety' my whole life and why I felt as if I had been alone since the age of three.

So now I ask the question; how did I, or how does anyone get to the 'Land of Anxiety'? I believe for me it started as a young boy when I was exposed to psychic reading parties at home. It was then that I was exposed to the occult and the fascination of wanting to know the future apart from God. So I began to inquire about the occult myself and started taking what might be considered small steps towards its practice. I engaged in forbidden and unproductive activities such as reading my daily horoscope, playing with Ouija boards and messing around with all kinds of occultist séances. From these practices grew within me an inclination to want to know and control my future.

During my teen years I also wore a gold necklace that had an Aquarius medallion on it and without even realizing it I was announcing to the world that I was the one in control of my future and not God! It is amazing to me how the Enemy can cloud someone's future at such an early age, but that's exactly what Satan did with me. He deceived me into believing the lie called the 'illusion of control'; if someone can actually see their future they can control it! And by 'see the future' I mean to picture it in your mind as you think it will happen without God! It will be full of all our 'What If's'. "What if God allows something bad to happen?" "What if God doesn't come through?" "What if God can't supply my needs?" and the always popular "What if things don't turn out the way I think they should?" Any or all of these 'What if's' will always lead to feelings of insecurity and cause us to try and take control of the future by picturing outcomes that don't factor in God. But as a young boy growing up without Christ I was defenseless against this onslaught of lies and fell victim early on.

Here's what I believe took this deception of the 'illusion of control' to a whole new level; it is a bridge, a backwards bridge that exists in the wasteland called the 'Mind Altered Bridge!' In order to cross this bridge you must go through a gateway and I assure you it's not the door of hope! This gateway is a door of hopelessness that leads to the demonic world. The way I opened this door was through the use of mind altering drugs; especially marijuana! Once I had crossed the 'Mind Altered Bridge' I found myself a permanent prisoner in the 'Land of anxiety'. No matter how hard I tried to escape, my addiction to marijuana led me to walk back over that backward bridge and go deeper into the captivity of fear and anxiety.

I started using marijuana in college right after I gave up on my dream of playing college football. Because of the devastation I felt deep down in my soul from surrendering my lifelong dream I decided to turn to marijuana in order to anesthetize the pain in my heart. So when the Lord saved me at the age of twenty-nine, the very first thing He asked me to do was stop smoking marijuana. He told me that if I wanted to live the life He had planned for me, smoking marijuana would have to end and never return. I would need to rely on Him **alone** for comfort. I quit that day and haven't considered its use since, even though the Enemy has tempted me many times.

Many who are reading this book right now are struggling with drugs, addictions and spiritual strongholds and feel as if there is no way out from that prison of hopelessness. Some may even be at the point where the only answer is to continue to anesthetize their hearts with more of the same; but there is a better way, Jesus Christ! "Do not get drunk on wine, which leads to debauchery; instead be filled with the Spirit..." (Ephesians 5:18). Brokenness allows us to invite Jesus into the process of deliverance from these strongholds, most of which we are powerless to conquer on our own. Only Jesus can deliver us from the Land of Anxiety, and our many rational and irrational fears. Lean on Him!

FEAR OF MAN

The fear that did the most damage to my hopes and dreams while living in the land of anxiety was the fear of man! It is a debilitating fear that will cause one to think irrationally and make bad decisions in every area of life. The one who fears man has shifted their trust away from God and given it to man and that's never a good thing. Let me tell you why! Psalm 118:8, reads that "It is better to take refuge in the Lord than to trust in man." Someone like me who has sought the darkest part of man (the occult) to discover what his future holds has the greatest chance of developing this fear. It's when you put man ahead of God for your immediate and future security that you open a door that allows this fear to rule in your heart!

All my life I feared what man could do to me. I bought the lie that certain men could determine what may or may not be allowed to happen in my life based on the degree of power and influence they carried in this world. I developed many tactics to defend myself from this fear. One of those defense tactics was people pleasing! People pleasers are more worried about what people think of them instead of what God thinks of them. Galatians 1:10 says it best, "Am I now trying to win the approval of human beings, or of God? Or am I trying to please people? If I were still trying to please people, I would not be a servant of Christ."

Because of my fear of man I had to master the art of people pleasing to cope with others and I believe it kept me from the life God had planned for me. And because people pleasing is so exhausting, a lifetime of it was finally bringing me to the end of my ability to defend myself with it. Towards the end of the summer of 2012 I began to grow desperate and I cried out to God to deliver me from my anxiety, which I believe was mostly caused by the fear of man. It had taken its toll on me and I was done. I begged God to do whatever it took to release me from the prison of anxiety so that I might finally be able to walk in the freedom Christ had died for on the cross. And answer the prayer he did!

The answer came in the form of a trial that lasted six months. It was a trial above my pay grade and far beyond my ability to cope but one planned by God in order to deal with my debilitating fear of man. The trial was in the realm of business where the fear of man can wield some of its most powerful work and cause a great deal of damage. But the way it ended was something for which I was not prepared.

But let me tell you, God knows what He is doing and thankfully He had a plan which included sending a helper to navigate me through this entire ordeal. Through his coaching and guidance I learned to lean on God's help through this trial. At first I felt anxious and vulnerable, but for the first time in my life I decided to cast my anxiousness completely unto God.

Two weeks before the end of this trail a close friend shared a verse with me that would change my life forever! Her bible study was memorizing scripture and she said she felt led to share the scriptures with me. The verses came from Hebrews 13: 5-6 and read as follows; "Keep your lives free from the love of money and be content with what you have, because God has said, "Never will I leave you; never will I forsake you." So we say with confidence,

"The Lord is my helper; I will not be afraid. What can man do to me?" At that moment I had no idea what these verses meant for my life, nor could I ever imagine how God was about to use their power to set me free. So I memorized the verses and was off to a meeting set by God to change the entire course of my life!

I headed to the meeting with no real expectations of what was to come out of it. I was somewhat distraught by the anxiousness of not knowing its outcome; another lingering effect of the fear of man. Upon entering the meeting room I immediately realized its set up was meant to be very intimidating and tried to pay it as little attention as possible. After several hours of what I felt to be an interrogation, the meeting came to its climax. It was here that I would be faced with my toughest decision ever; "Do I continue to trust in man or do I finally put my trust in God?"

At one point I was given an ultimatum that if agreed upon would put me at in a precarious situation for the rest of my life; it was an ultimatum that I rejected! At that moment I had a sense that the only way I could accept the proposals of this ultimatum would be for me to do so out of fear! So it became the turning point at which I finally decided not to back down to man anymore and take the first step in my quest for the freedom from the fear of man. But my rejection of the ultimatum led to a verbal outburst from the other party that would last for several minutes! Let me tell you, it was so loud and aggressive that I felt the slap of every word on my face as well as having my hair blown back! It took me to a place and degree of fear that I had never been to before. I was absolutely terrified and somewhat paralyzed from the fear. Now my initial thoughts were; "I am going to get up and grab my topcoat off the back of the chair, wave goodbye and talk to my lawyer." And as I began to turn my shoulder in the direction of my overcoat I heard a voice say my name and I thought to myself, "Did I just hear that?" And what really amazed me most about the voice was the clarity and softness of it in the midst of the outrage! I could hear both of the voices simultaneously but the soft, quiet whisper of this unseen voice smothered the rage of the other voices' outburst. I knew right then that it was God, but I was still having a hard time believing I could hear His voice so clearly, especially in the midst of the screaming.

It was at that moment that God and I had a conversation and it went like this; ME..."Is that you God? GOD...Yes it is! ME... This is crazy! I am so scared and I'm on my way out! GOD... I know you are. I put you here on purpose by orchestrating all of this especially for you. This is neither an accident nor simply a set of circumstances. It is all my doing and it is for your best! ME... But I think he wants to devour me? GOD... Maybe, but I am in total control... So let me present you with a choice; you can get up, put your topcoat on, and walk out that door; Or, you can sit right here in my lap resting in me and watch as I battle on your behalf? (Remember Hebrews 13; 5-6!) But before you answer let me reveal to you the eventual outcomes. If you choose to leave you will remain a prisoner to the fear of man for the rest of your life! Choosing to stay and allowing me to fight this battle on your behalf will deliver you from the fear of man and open your eyes to the freedom you already have in my son Jesus! What will it be? Will you choose to put your trust in me rather than man?!!! ME... I am so scared Lord! But I am in! I will put my trust in you! GOD... Well done! Sit now quietly and do not speak, I will do the rest!

Wow! What I witnessed next was nothing short of a miracle! I sat there without speaking a word for the next forty-five minutes and watched God change the other party's heart around one hundred and eighty degrees from their original position. It was absolutely amazing! I never said a word and when the meeting ended after two hours and forty-five minutes I walked out of there with every penny I was owed, an apology, and a handshake! I left that meeting with everything I desired and with everything that every person I spoke with told me I wasn't going to get! God came through as He promises to come through; 'Exceedingly and abundantly more than we can ever ask or imagine!' What a huge step in my quest to be free from fear and anxiety. The fear of man was struck a death blow in my life and with it would come another major benefit; it would take with it the love of money!

One of the biggest problems with the fear of man is that it leads to the love of money! They are both so intricately intertwined and extremely hard to separate. You rarely see one without the other and that's because those who fear man will always look to money as their security instead of God! Fear of man leads us to believe that if we somehow can make enough and save enough money we will finally be secure! We will finally be safe from and at peace with this fallen and broken world! I have now come to understand the lie that the Enemy uses to enslave us to the fear of man; 'make enough money and all your troubles will be gone!' Don't believe it!

Living at peace in this world comes from only one source; the Cross! That is why Jesus promises us His peace and not that of man, money or the things of this world. John 14:27, "Peace I (Jesus) leave with you; my peace I give you. I do not give as the world gives. Do not let your hearts be troubled and do not be afraid." Wow! Two freedoms for the price of one trial, that's a heavenly deal!

FIGHTING FROM VICTORY

Besides the freedoms I realized from the trial just stated, I also had my eyes opened to another very powerful truth; 'No more fighting for victory, we fight from victory!' As I look back upon that six month trial I realize now that it was perfectly orchestrated by God in His perfect timing. He did it in order to offend my mind and capture my heart! But what does it mean for God to 'Offend our minds in order to capture our hearts?' Let me explain. The mind is the battlefield to capture the heart because our thoughts develop our beliefs. It means that God is more interested in what we love and therefore believe, than what we think or know! We cannot worship and follow God with our minds; it must be with our hearts! Romans 10:10 says, "For it is with your heart that you believe and are justified, and it is with your mouth that you profess your faith and are saved."

Just knowing who God is and what His promises are, without believing in your heart and living by faith produces an empty life that is void of God's miracles! Remember Hebrews 11:1, "Now faith is confidence in what we hope for and assurance about what we do not see." Faith believes in the promises of God that we cannot see with our natural eyes! I knew what Hebrews 13: 5-6 said, but I had never believed it to be true before I walked through that trial. Knowing that God knows all my needs and will never leave me or forsake me did no good in my life till I actually experienced that truth in the midst of that trial. That is why God specifically orchestrated that trial for me at this point in my life. He knew my ability and desire to defend myself from man had run its course and it was time for me to get promoted to a life of faith in God! You see, 'courage is a demonstration of faith.' And there is no true courage without real fear. Therefore, I had to be put in a terrifying situation to experience real fear in order to develop true courage! God was teaching me to fight 'from victory' and not 'for victory'! The victory spoken of here was won at the cross when Jesus defeated Satan once and for all.

There is no longer any need to fight this world for that victory, the fight is over; "It is finished!" Someone who fights 'from victory' instead of 'for victory' has the courage to trust God in the midst of real danger. We as believers are going to face real danger in this life. The apostle Paul speaks of this in Romans chapter 8 as he quotes Psalm 44:22, "Yet for your sake we face death all day long; we are considered as sheep to be slaughtered." He then responds with the next verse, "No, in all these things we are more than conquerors through him who loved us." We are more than conquerors because the battle has already been won at the cross! God was preparing me for a life of faith and this trial was my promotion to it. That is why we are told to 'take up our cross daily', so we can fight spiritually from a position of victory and grace and not fight for something we already have and could never achieve on our own.

So the battle to renew my mind from a life time of defeat and loss under the fear of man was well under way and the Lord was in total control. The battle is mine says the Lord! And now that my trust had been transferred from man and restored back to God, the original and rightful owner, I was in a position for God to begin the next phase in the restoration process of my life. This would include reclaiming all territory the Enemy had captured from me as a result of my trusting in man! I was about to receive a very precious gift, Hope!

DAY I DISCOVERED HOPE

Last year I was introduced to a bridge called 'Hopesteration'. It would be the bridge God would walk me across to restore hope back into my life! We all know by reading 1st Corinthians chapter 13 that there are three abiding realities of the Christian life; Faith, Hope and Love. The past two years of my life's journey have been leading me towards a God centered hope and away from the false hope this world promises us; which I call wishful thinking! In order to obtain true hope I believe that there must be a scriptural basis to stand on and I believe it is found in Romans 8:28,

"And we know that in all things God works for the good of those who love Him, who have been called according to His purpose." If we truly believe that everything in our life has been orchestrated by God and for our best including the good and the bad we should never despair no matter what our circumstances may be. King David spoke of this hope in Psalm 27:13 (NASB) when he declared, "*I would have despaired* unless I had believed that I would see the goodness of the Lord in the land of the living."

David's hope was in God and he believed God was in control and would work all things together for good; even David's mistakes and acts of disobedience, which were plenty! Therefore, David had hope! He wasn't hopeless which leads to desperation. That's why he said he *would have despaired*, been distraught and even fearful, had he not believed God was in control and working every circumstance out for the good. And that is exactly what God taught me in the trial I previously shared concerning my deliverance from the fear of man. He taught me that He was sovereign and in total control of every person and every circumstance. It is stated in Proverbs 21:1, "The King's heart is in the hand of the Lord, as are the watercourses; He turns it whichever way He wills." This verse tells us that everyone and everything on this earth is ultimately controlled by God. This is not saying that we don't have a mind and will of our own, along with the freedom to choose; it simply means that God's in control of everything! That is the foundation to having Hope; knowing and believing that God is in total control and working everything out for the good! Loving God and walking out the purpose to which He has called us are the requirements to experience Hope!

So this summer as I traveled throughout the east coast, I was lead to a prayer from the Apostle Paul to the Ephesians (1:18), "I pray that the eyes of your heart may be enlightened in order that you may know the **hope** to which he has called you, the riches of his glorious inheritance in his holy people." God was beginning to open the eyes of my heart to see and believe in a God centered hope, a hope that I had never experienced before in life! The revealing of hope to me began while I was traveling home from Greenville, SC one summer day in June when I realized I was actually on another bridge; the one from 'A Wasteland pessimist to a Garden optimist!' Wow! I began to notice for the first time in my life I was seeing the cup as half full and not half empty. I began to see that whatever my circumstance, it was intended for the good by God. Let me explain this by introducing to you the 'Wasteland Pessimist'. This guy has been corrupted and polluted by the world. He loves money and has an inherent fear of man which can be masked by self-confidence, drive, ambition or simply just wanting a better life. He has it all including the car, the house, the beautiful wife and he's living the 'good life' because his greed has made him rich by the world's standards. Now all these 'things' aren't necessarily bad or wrong per se, it is when they are pursued and obtained with the wrong motive and used for one's own glory that they become stumbling blocks. He knows if things are going to get done he will have to do them himself. I have seen this guy before in the mirror (minus the wife)!

Now let me introduce to you the 'Garden Optimist'. This guy knows that God loves him and that God has his back because he has given his heart fully to Him. He knows that all things whether good, bad or indifferent work for the good of God's kingdom and His purpose. He knows that God will meet his every need so he no longer needs to run out ahead of God and make as much money as possible so that his future will be safe and secure. His security is in Christ and the cross! He walks with God, eats with God and then rests with God. So my path to hope was becoming a whole lot brighter each and every passing moment and I began to sense this new hope on the horizon!

I continued my travels for the summer taking most of the month of July off and splitting the time between a farm in SC and the beach in NC. The beach was a time of relaxing with good friends that included boating, fishing and lots of good meals. I enjoyed every minute of my time at the beach and had no desire to leave. The farm was also a place of fun and restoration, although it entailed some work but it was the kind of work I enjoyed and makes you sleep like a baby! I relished every minute of it and had no desire to leave there as well. My month long vacation had finally reached its conclusion. So I said goodbye to the farm and began my journey home on a Sunday morning, July 14th, a day I will never forget!

As I pulled out onto the road and began a five hour ride home I was filled with gratitude in my heart and began to just thank God and praise Him for the amazing time I had this summer. But while in the midst of worshipping God on my drive, I looked out through the windshield and saw the largest and most beautiful double rainbow. These two rainbows looked like hand painted archways on display from heaven itself! I suddenly remembered that I had seen three other rainbows while at the beach and on the farm, so these were actually rainbows four and five that I had seen on my vacation; Five rainbows! I had a sense that Jesus put those rainbows in the sky that day specifically for me. They were a sign to me that Grace abounded in my life and that He (Jesus) was that Grace. Then, all of sudden I felt God's presence like never before and finally came to the realization that I truly belonged to Him. His covenant with me to never leave me or forsake me could not be broken. I could see His love and protection hovering over me in the rainbows; they represented God's love and protection for me! And then it hit me, "I have HOPE!" July 14th 2013 was the day that I discovered hope! I was finally content with my life and its circumstances and confident that God was in total control for the first time in my life. I realized I was content at the beach, I was content working on the farm and I was content with the fact I needed to get back to Atlanta and work. I was truly content! I remember saying to myself at that moment, "So this is what contentment feels like!" Wow! Now I have hope! And hope being 'a confident expectation of good to oneself', I realized that life will never be the same for me now that I have discovered hope. My perspective on life had been completely turned around from 'a Wasteland Pessimist to a Garden Optimist!' I actually experienced hope for the first time in my life deep down in my heart! I started to believe that good was on its way, and there was no need to run out ahead of God and try to control my future any longer. I had just received one of the greatest desires of my heart and greatest gifts in this world; Hope!!!

Why is it so important for us to have hope? Jesus as our good Sheppard promises us He will restore our souls (will, mind and emotions). King David spoke of this restoration in Psalm 23:3 "He (Jesus) restores my soul;" Restoration means getting something back to its original condition. That is exactly what God's intention is for the soul trapped in the wasteland. It is to restore the soul back to its original condition. We are given hope as part of the restoration of our soul. Hope is the foundation, or should I say 'anchor of our soul'. Hebrews 6:19 says, "We have this hope as an anchor for the soul, firm and secure." Why do we need 'Hope' as an anchor? Well, let me give you an example. Boats need anchors because they are made to float on water. If they are not anchored down to something firm and secure they will be at the mercy of the water; susceptible to being tossed to and fro by its waves. We too need an anchor to survive in this fallen, broken and unstable world. Hope is that anchor for a believer that passes through this temporal, unstable and insecure world to the eternal where Jesus lives. Our hope is in Jesus and what He did at the cross. Hope is the anchor for our souls which keeps our hearts from be tossed to and fro from the uncertainties and fears of life in this world. With hope as the anchor to my soul I now have my security in Christ and it can no longer be tossed back and forth by the lies of the Enemy!

What I have also discovered about hope is that it's essential to having God give us His best for our lives! Without hope God will often withhold or delay His best from us because He knows we won't be able to appreciate it in our current state of hopelessness. That is because I have come to believe that the one thing God hates is indifference! I discovered that in reading the story of Jacob and Esau, Isaac's two sons. Esau the oldest gave up his birthright as the first born son, a huge blessing in the Jewish culture, to satisfy his hunger pangs. It was his indifference toward the blessings of God that enabled him to give up his birthright for a bowl of stew! Esau did not appreciate what God had given him and gave it away! Hopelessness leads to indifference! Nothing is more painful than to witness someone who has sabotaged the very best of what God has given them because of their indifference toward it. Those without hope will walk away from marriages and families, careers and so many other blessings of God simply because they were indifferent to them in the first place. Indifferent people will also be skeptical and at times push blessings away or even run from them because it will seem too good to be true. Hopelessness says things like; what's the catch? What if it turns out not to be a good thing? When will I lose it? Is it a test? What's the use? Didn't want or need it anyway! There are so many ways to sabotage God's best without hope. That is how the 'Wasteland Pessimist' thinks, he's indifferent. His thoughts are always on what might go wrong, or what he may lose. He lives life with his hands clenched tightly together holding on to everything he thinks he needs which prevents him from grabbing hold of God's best.

Hope allows us to receive! Hope gives us a grateful and appreciative heart like Jacob, the other brother in this story. Jacob appreciated what God had to offer and was shrewd enough and willing to work hard and did whatever it took to receive the best God had to offer! When we have hope as the anchor to our soul, the stability and security we receive from that will cause appreciation to flourish within our hearts! This allows us to open our hands and our hearts to God without fear and receive His best; whatever that may be! The 'Garden Optimist' is full of hope and opens his entire life to God because he is confidently expecting good! He has been put in a position to be blessed because he appreciates all God has to offer. His desire is for God's best! I never want to live with indifference again and thankfully because of hope I won't have to!

BECOMING GOD'S BEST

Immediately following my discovery of hope another truth was revealed to me that opened my eyes further into the restoration of my soul. As I began to live my life with new found hope I started to notice something about people, especially believers. This caused me to stop and meditate on one of my favorite scriptures Proverbs 20:11, "Even a child is known by his actions by whether his conduct is pure and right." You might ask; what does this verse have to do with restoration? Well I asked the same question and here is what I discovered and it is a powerful truth. "Watch and learn from how people live their life!" I have begun paying more attention in life now to people's actions. We so often want to be known as someone who extends grace, or gives the benefit of the doubt, or looks for the good in others that we often leave our hearts wide open to destruction. Now I am not saying that those previous traits are wrong, they are all good traits when extended with discernment and not naivety.

Let me explain. In 1st Kings 3:7, King Solomon is speaking before God as a young King in need of direction and wisdom to rule Israel. Verse 7 reads, "Now, Lord my God, you have made your servant king in place of my father David. But I am only a child and do not know how to carry out my duties." Solomon expressed to God that he was given great responsibility but did not have the wisdom or discernment yet to carry out his calling. Solomon felt as if he was still a little child who was not prepared to rule as a man or a king. So he then decides to do what few are willing to do, he asks God to give him a discerning heart! 1st kings 3:9 then reads (Solomon speaking), "So give your servant a discerning heart to govern your people and to distinguish between right and wrong…" Solomon realized what God wants us all to realize; that in order live out our life calling we will need a discerning (pure and sensitive) heart in order to discern between what is right and wrong, Gods best and ours, and the difference between truth and deception. One of the first benefits of a discerning heart is the ability to discern the truth by watching how people live their lives. Just as hope anchors our soul to the truth, discernment protects that hope by identifying what is true. Discernment is the protector of hope!

We need to protect our hope because there is a battle taking place within. The Enemy does not want God to restore the hearts and souls of men because those whose hearts are restored through hope become dangerous to his evil plan. So Satan will continually attack our hearts at two main gates; the eye gate and the ear gate. What we listen to and what we watch are extremely important to the outcome of this battle. The Enemy gets in to our mind when we give him permission through what we listen to and watch. Be careful little children as to what you see and hear! Part of the journey to the garden requires cultivating a pure and sensitive heart to God. So once hope is restored to our life I believe God immediately begins to give us discernment to close and protect the gates of our hearts. And that is why I began looking at people and life so differently. I noticed that the majority of people I encountered (including myself) talked of wanting God's best and becoming the person God wanted them to be, but few were actually living their lives in such a way to achieve that. Then the true meaning of a popular saying became a whole lot clearer to me, "If it were easy everyone would be doing it!" Obtaining wisdom and discernment along with cultivating a pure and sensitive heart is not an easy task; it requires brokenness! Once we are broken we must then surrender of our entire lives to God, along with all our agenda's and plans for the future and finally have the willingness to let God have complete control of our life's purpose. It's a tough call for anyone to respond to, but one I believe I (we) now have the 'hope' to fulfill!

TIME TO GROW UP

If I truly want to become the man of God I desire to be and the man God has purposed me to be, I believe it is time that I grow up and in order to do so God would introduce me to another bridge that was needed to be crossed; the one from 'A Childish boy to A Childlike man'. I have to admit this bridge was an eye opener for me that I didn't see coming. But it makes perfect sense now as I step back and look at my life up until now. This bridge was revealed to me in August this year after a meeting with a dear friend and mentor. I shared with him what I felt was happening deep down in my heart and the direction I thought God was leading. I'll never forget his response; "You are Root-Bound". Root-Bound is a horticulture term that refers to a plant in a pot that is too small. It needs to be uprooted and re-planted in a bigger pot so that it can be nourished and grow. I was that plant! I needed to be uprooted from my comfortable surroundings, security blankets and safety nets. They were all hindering my growth because I tended to go to them first before seeking God. If I were going to continue this journey to the center of the garden I was going to have to begin living my entire life as a man relying on God first; I would have to grow from a childish boy into a childlike man! It was apparent to me now that several areas of my life were stuck in the childish boy stage and were in need of some growing up!

That is exactly what happened the very next day. I became aware that there was a spirit of confusion in me and that it had a stronghold in my heart ever since I was a young boy. This somewhat explains why I feel as if I have been completely alone since the age of three. But again God knew when enough was enough and so I said goodbye to that spirit of confusion that kept me a 'Childish Boy' and stepped onto to this new bridge leading to a 'Childlike Man' and began to walk with confidence for the first time in my life. But in order to experience the full growth of this bridge I was going to have to be uprooted and placed into a temporary place before I could be re-planted into a new environment and that is exactly what happened. Six weeks later is when I made the decision to spend the next year in Wrightsville Beach NC. After 25 years in Atlanta, GA where I had developed a very comfortable life, I was now going to be in an unfamiliar place where all my comforts would be stripped away. I would have to lean on God more than I ever have before. This was new territory for me and a bit scary, but because of my new found hope and faith it was finally possible for me to follow God without knowing what was future held. I was now confident that whatever God had in store for me would ultimately work for the good and I was going to have to live by faith and not sight if I wanted to experience God's best. It is something I have not done very well before in life. I've always said that I don't mind walking on water; I just need to know where the rocks are!

So as I began the journey across this bridge I asked God a question; what does a childlike man look like? "I'm glad you asked!" replied God. I believe now as I start to learn the discipline of hearing God's voice that I am afforded the luxury of learning from God in a much more expedient way. Being present is the only way to receive instruction from God before the journey begins. Learning the ways of God while living out ahead of Him in the land of anxiety will cause one to endure many trials and tribulations. It is why I have suffered through so many trials in my life. I've always run out ahead of God just like a little boy would do wanting to show his parents that he knows the way and can do or find whatever himself. I've always meant well trying to help God out by running ahead of Him, but I lacked maturity and therefore suffered much tribulation along the way. Proverbs 19:2 warns us of this, "It is not good to have zeal without knowledge, nor to be hasty and miss the way." Not only is it not good, it can really hurt sometimes!

So as God and I started walking together on this bridge He graciously began revealing to me the characteristics of a childlike man. Here is what I believe God revealed to me as the seven pillars of a childlike man; 1) He responds to God immediately! There is no hesitation in his obedience because he believes that God is for him. 2) He is weak before God, but strong before men! This characteristic will develop as a result of being loosed from the fear of man. 3) He doesn't remain in immaturity for life! He has graduated from the classroom of restoration and healing and stepped out onto the road of life. 4) He waits for the Lord! (He lives by faith moment by moment) He has transferred his trust from man unto God. 5) He communes with God on a continual basis! He knows this will lead to an intimate relationship with Jesus and that He will bless him with quality of life. 6) He willingly receives all that God has for him! This includes the good and the bad. 7) He invites God into every area of his life! He holds nothing back from God and nothing in his life is off limits (sex, money, marriage…

nothing!). Ask and you shall receive! I believe these 7 pillars are a rock solid foundation placed in my heart to help me cross this bridge. I can't wait to see the benefits these characteristics will bring to my life as they take root and grow within my heart.

I've waited for this bridge a very long time, almost twenty years! I began to dream about it a year after God saved me. I would read 1st Corinthians 13 every day trying to understand what love truly was. Thanks to a patient God this chapter of the bible is beginning to blossom in my heart. I realize now that as I read that chapter a thousand times over the seeds were being planted in hopes that one day the soil of my heart would be healthy enough for them to grow! You see, and I quote 1st Corinthians 13:11; "When I was a child, I talked like a child; I thought like a child, I reasoned like a child. When I became a man, I put childish ways behind me." Putting these childish ways of mine behind me on this bridge is going to allow me to get to the center of the garden where childlike men of God live. Again, I'm on my way!

KEY OF DAVID

In order to ignite my maturation process into high gear God would have to begin a process of closing all the wrong doors that I had opened in my life while living in the wasteland. These were doors that allowed the Enemy access to my life and where he then could inflict some severe mental, emotional and physical damage. Enough damage to keep me enslaved to fear like a childish little boy. I needed to be set free from these bad influences for the journey ahead.

It was then that I was introduced to a biblical term called the 'Key of David!' Throughout this year as I counseled with a mentor of mine a continual theme would surface. "Closing the doors to my past" It seemed as if God were leading me back to people and places where I was either wounded or had allowed something into my life that was spiritually detrimental to my growth. It became apparent that God was closing every door I had opened which allowed Satan entry into my heart and mind. This was not an easy process. I came to the realization that it is extremely difficult to regain the stolen territory of one's heart which was once Satan's stronghold. I know the Enemy has strongholds in me and I have tried for twenty years to break them in my own effort never to succeed. But something was different this year. This was the year I surrendered that task to God. He is the only one capable of breaking the strongholds and kicking the Enemy out while shutting the door behind him.

After about eight months of going through the process of having doors shut in my life that were harmful to me, I heard a sermon in August that confirmed everything. It was a message on the 'Year of the Key of David!' The speaker went on to share that this was the year God would be closing all doors that are harmful to his followers as well as opening new doors that would lead us to the purposes of our lives. That is exactly what I had been experiencing so far this year!

An important mention of God closing a door in the bible is in Genesis when Moses is describing the process of filling up Noah's ark with all the animals and his family. Once Noah had gotten everything and everyone into the ark, Genesis 7:16 says, "… Then the Lord shut him in." Hmmm…! It was God who shut the door to the ark and not Noah as I had always believed. The door was too big for Noah to shut. Only God could shut the door to the ark and He did it to protect those inside from the danger about to be unleashed outside. It is the same for our lives as well. There are certain doors that only God can shut, particularly the ones to the demonic world which we have allowed to open. We simply don't have the strength or ability to shut them ourselves, but they must be closed to protect us from the strongholds of the Enemy.

The 'Key of David' itself comes from the book of Isaiah and is a metaphor used in the prophecy of the Davidic Messiah (meaning the Messiah would come from the bloodline of King David) suggesting that Christ is the only one who can grant access to God. In other words the Key of David is the 'Key' of all keys and can do what no other ordinary key can do. This key is also mentioned in the book of Revelation 3:7, where the apostle John was instructed to write a letter to the church in Philadelphia, it says; "To the church in Philadelphia write: These are the words of him who is holy and true, who holds the key of David. What he opens no one can shut, and what he shuts no one can open." So there it is! When God decides enough is enough and begins the process of restoring our souls by shutting doors that we should not have opened in the first place there is no man, beast or foul spirit that can open them again unless we give them permission.

GOODBYE TO THE SCUMBAG

In September of (2013), I finally decided to rent a house on Wrightsville beach and ponder a possible permanent move out of Atlanta. I believe it was part of God's plan to deliver me from my 'Root-Bound' stage. I was going to sign a one year lease and see what might come of it. I found a house which had Banks Channel as its back yard. It had an amazing view that would allow me to watch the sun set every night from the dock that overlooked the bay. It seemed like the perfect set up for me and the beginning of a new journey. But then it hit me! These waters were a link to my past! It was the part of my life that I was not proud of deep down inside. It actually made me feel like a Scumbag! Let me explain.

When I was in college in the mid-eighties I developed the habit of smoking marijuana to anesthetize all the pain in my heart. That habit combined with my desire to be an entrepreneur like my dad lead to a perfect match; Drug dealer! I started off slow like everyone else does in small business, but quickly realized I was good at what I did and it grew into a flourishing operation. As my connections grew, I finally came up with the perfect strategy to get the product at the lowest possible price. I decided to work with just one individual (keep exposure and risk to minimal) and make the exchange of money and goods myself. My supplier, who resided in Wrightsville beach at that time, and I would meet halfway between Greenville North Carolina and the beach to make our monthly exchange at an abandoned carwash. It would look as if we were two guys looking to clean our cars. It was there that we made the exchange, my cash for his weed. I did this for about two years before it was time for me to graduate and go get a real job! But what I failed to realize was the guilt that the Enemy would have me carry deep down in my soul for the next twenty-five years! It was an ever so silent guilt but its whispers could condemn me at any time, any place and with anyone!

For the next twenty-five years, even after being born again and becoming a brand new creation in Christ, I still felt condemned by the guilt of breaking the law and flooding a campus of students with a harmful mind altering drug. This condemnation would tell me that I can't ever succeed in real business; I only know how to cheat like a scumbag. I can't really trust anyone as a true friend because I'm (the drug dealer) not trustworthy. I'm a scumbag! I can't even get married to a good Christian girl because I have no character. Drug dealers are lacking in the area of character, and I'm a scumbag! On and on it would go for decades. But as you know, I serve a God who is all about redemption and I was about to have my soul redeemed!

Here's where things get interesting. You see, the water way in the backyard of this beach house is known as Banks Channel. This is the water way where the marijuana I sold was delivered from South America. Back then the drug runners would drop barrels in the water that were loaded with pounds of marijuana tightly sealed and waterproof. My connections would recover the weed and sell it to guys like me, who in turn would sell it to smaller dealers and end users. Therefore Banks Channel was the origin of my drug dealing days. It was the point where drugs entered this country and my life. It was where the door to this lifestyle was opened and it needed to be shut. So then I began to realize that God was taking me back to the place where condemnation entered my soul and His plan was to shut the door that allowed the enemy access. But first he would have to deal with the 'Scumbag' that lived down in there. His removal would precede the closing of the door! What happened next was pretty cool.

A few weeks prior to actually renting the house on the beach I reached out to my mentor and told him that I was looking to rent a house for the next year that overlooked the waters where I used to get all my drugs in college. I told him that I felt like there was more to me renting that house then I could put my finger on. So we decided that since my move to Wrightsville beach was a huge event in my life and that there was more to this move than I originally thought that he would fly to Wilmington for a weekend of redemption; just me, him and God praying into this new adventure.

And so it began. He landed on a Friday night and by Saturday morning he and I were at the docks where the drugs would come ashore in Banks Channel and we invited God to open our eyes to whatever He had in store. It was there that things got quite unbelievable. As we started to pray an older gentlemen came walking down the dock with a fishnet in hand looking to cast the net in the shallows for baitfish. He looked worn and defeated as he aimlessly walked the docks hunched over with little confidence of finding what he was looking for. And then it struck me, that's what the enemy made me feel like when he would heap piles of condemnation on me. It left me feeling defeated, hunched over and lost. It made me feel like a loser scumbag! Like someone who didn't deserve to have any desires of the heart come to fruition. Like someone walking this journey of life aimlessly without hope, all because I decided to deal drugs in college. In the Enemy's eyes I was disillusioned to think God would ever bless someone like me. So in the name of Jesus, we asked God to shut the door to my past and lock all its baggage away forever! I'll never forget what happened next. Seconds after we prayed this prayer an employee from a nearby restaurant came out the back door with a large black garbage bag full of trash, went over to a pickup truck and threw the garbage in the bed of the truck. He then reached up and slammed the hatch shut. It was right then and there that I knew all the baggage I was carrying, the guilt, shame and condemnation from my drug dealer days were being thrown into the abyss and that door in my life was permanently shut. But that wasn't all; we were just beginning the day!

We then hopped into the car and began to drive toward the abandoned carwash where I would meet my connection. It was about an hour and fifteen minute drive and we prayed the entire way asking God to close every door the enemy had used to bring illicit drugs into my life. As we drove we could hear doors closing all along the way. Then we finally arrived at the carwash and slowly made our way to the back where I had parked my car so many times to make deals. I got out alone to have some time with God and just to soak up all the emotions that were running through my head and heart. It was so crazy to be there again. It just about took my breath away! Several minutes later he got out of the car and we began to ask God to again open our eyes to His purpose for this stop; and WOW!!! Did He ever open my eyes! In the middle of our prayer I noticed that one of the car wash vacuum cylinders was unlocked. I then heard this still small quiet voice say to me; close the cylinder door and lock it. I instantly knew it was the Holy Spirit. I reached over and shut the door, clamped down the lock and felt the weight of my drug dealing years fall off. The doorway of illicit drugs which the Enemy used to enter and corrupt my life was closed and locked up forever! What an amazing experience and tremendous relief. As if that wasn't enough, when I looked up to thank God for what had just happened I saw a lamp post in the shape of a cross hovering above. It was at that moment I realized that God was always here watching over me, even when I was a college age scumbag there only to pick up drugs. I just didn't know it. He protected me then, and He has redeemed me from it now! Can it possibly get any better; yep!!!

So while we were still in amazement, we got in the car and proceeded to our final stop; the house where I lived and dealt drugs from for two years. It was another hour and a half drive and we continued to pray that God would close any other doors and strongholds to the past. We also asked him to show us the purpose for going back to that house. When we arrived we parked right in front of the house. It was there sitting there in the car that I could hear that quiet voice whispering to me, "Go knock on the door!" I was a little nervous but thought it sounded like a pretty cool idea. But what would I say if someone answered the door? It would be totally awkward, yet I felt compelled to do it. We both agreed I should do it alone and I did so while he waited in the car. So off I went. I walked up and knocked on the screen door hoping no one would answer. After about ten seconds I could hear the door opening. A college age young man answered and said, "Can I help you?" It took me a second but I caught my breath and told him I used to live at this house twenty-five years ago while I was a student in college and wanted to show my buddy where I used to live. He was okay about it and even thought it was a cool that I would want to stop by after such a long period of time. But here is what took this part of the journey to a whole new level. I asked him if I could peak my head inside to see what it looked like after so many years.

The outside was the same, but I wanted to see if anything had changed inside. He said sure and let me look inside and my jaw just about hit the floor! I mean it was exactly like it was when I was there twenty-five years ago. There was another young man sitting on the couch and these two guys were getting high! They were having a "session", getting "baked!" They were sitting in the dark smoking their time away in a fog, the exact thing I was doing twenty-five years ago in the exact same room of the exact same house. So God quickly said to me to take a good look at my past and the darkness and isolation that life brought me say goodbye to it! Goodbye to that weed smoking, drug dealing dude who sat in a dark living room throughout college, missing out on those precious years. Say "Goodbye to the Scumbag!" And that's what I did! I then thanked the young man for allowing me to look inside. I shook his hand and turned to walk away. As I did I heard the word, "Listen", whispered in my ear. And the next thing I heard was the door being shut, "Boom!" It was all over. The day's journey down the corridor of my drug dealing past had ended with the final door closed. I was free and my life of learning to live as a loved person was going to the next level. We then sat down to some good NC barbeque and drove home. It was a peaceful drive this time. The car was a lot lighter as well because of all the baggage I dropped off.

As God continues to shut doors in my life that are harmful to my soul, I also believe that He is opening new doors for me to grow and prosper on my journey. Revelation 3:8 tells us, "I know your deeds. See, I have placed before you an open door that no one can shut. I know that you have little strength, yet you have kept my word and have not denied my name." I believe for those committed to God, who don't shrink back or give up on Him (Hebrews 10: 36-39), He promises us an amazing journey to the center of the garden. He promises to open every door necessary for us to walk through and fulfill our purpose in life. Our responsibility is to keep walking towards those new doors of hope while crossing every necessary bridge as well. Once we get to these new open doors we must walk through with confidence knowing that God himself has opened them for us! This year there were also several new bridges that I would begin to cross in order to get to and walk through new doors.

NEW HOUSE NEW HEART

This is the bridge I believe will change the way I live more than any other I've encountered so far in my journey to the center of the garden. It is the bridge from an 'Uncommitted Heart to a Committed Heart'. It was given to me as a gift to help me stay the course and fulfill the purpose to which I have been called. That purpose is to glorify God and using my life as an example to point others to the cross! And although this is the newest and most recent bridge in my life journey it already has made a major impact in the way I think and live. Let me share how it was shown to me!

After signing the lease for my house in Wrightsville Beach I was given a move in date of Friday October 4th, 2013. It was that morning of the 4th while packing my car with my belongings that I began to experience heavy anxiety. I was moving all my stuff from a friend's house in Wilmington where I had been staying for a couple of weeks to my new place at the beach. Suddenly I started choking on anxiety! It was squeezing my chest and throat to the point I thought I was going to pass out. As I began to drive over the Causeway Bridge from Wilmington to the beach the anxiety grew worse. In order to cope I began to do what I do best; I started to plan my escape routes! Thoughts came to my mind like, "If it doesn't work out I still have Atlanta!" "If I don't find enough clients here I will just change my career!" "If this move crashes and burns, who can I go live with?" "Maybe I can marry rich and this will all go away!" and of course, "I think I made a mistake! What have I done?!!! Lord, show me the escape routes because the claustrophobia is setting in and I can't breathe!"

That was how my mind had been trained to think since I was a little boy: when scared run. The glass was always half empty and had a leak! First you panic and then find the escape route and run for your life! It is an awful and exhausting way to live. It is wasteland survival mode at best! But there is a huge lesson I've learned from my brokenness and that is; anxiety is a lie that only exists in my mind out in the future ahead of God and the plan He has for my life today. So now when anxiety tries to steal my joy I have trained myself to stop my thoughts and bring them back to the present moment and ask the question, "What lie do I believe right now to cause this fear?" That is exactly what I did and immediately the anxiety began to ease. It did not totally go away but I knew help was on its way. Here is what happened next!

Soon after I brought the last of my things into my new digs on the beach and checked out the spectacular views of the ocean and inlet from my front and back porches, I plugged in my computer and tried to get settled in. It was now about three hours from the time I cried out to God asking for wisdom to reveal the lie I believed was causing my anxiety. Feeling a little isolated out on the tiny little beach island I decided to get on social media and see what others were up to. As I scrolled down the news feed I came across a post that has and will forever change my life. It read as follows; "A committed heart looks for solutions, while an uncommitted heart looks for an escape." POW!!!! Down to my knees I went! I wasn't sure if I just got hit in the head, heart, nose or stomach, but down I went, and so did a lifetime of living with an uncommitted heart! I knew instantaneously that the emotions I was experiencing along with the events of this day were perfectly orchestrated by God in order for me to receive the revealing of this new bridge from a 'Uncommitted Heart' to a 'Committed Heart!' But not just the events of this day, this entire year and the past several years' events as well as my entire life's events were orchestrated by God to bring me to this place and time to receive this revelation!

Think about what God did just this year alone to get me here. He shut down the one company I had that tied me to Atlanta, sold my house I lived in for twelve years, cut all other permanent ties in Atlanta and found me a really cool house at the beach isolated from almost everything and everyone just to get me alone with Him so He could teach me this invaluable life lesson! That is to me "The Ruthless Love of God" for His children. God's love for us is ruthless because He is a jealous God! So jealous for His own that he will go to whatever means necessary to give us His best, even to the point of sacrificing His own son on a cross! That's GOD!!!

So now with my heart expanding like the Grinch's on top of Who 'Ville Mountain, I looked to God and asked Him a few necessary questions the way a son would ask his father. "Papa, what does it look like to live with a committed heart?" "What lies do I believe that cause me to look for escape routes instead of solutions?" "Papa, will you teach me to have a committed heart?"

What happened next was just simply amazing! Before the day was through God had impressed on my heart to take advantage of the ocean views and to meet Him in the mornings in one of my front rooms to watch the sunrise off the ocean. I thought to myself, "This is going to be a show!" I couldn't wait to sit with God and watch Him raise the sun right out of the horizon and off the ocean's surface! So I awoke the next morning to have my quiet time at sunrise and as I got to the room where I could see the ocean, I noticed that it was a pretty cloudy morning. Then I wondered if there would even be a sunrise because of the heavy cloud cover but I decided to just sit there quietly and patiently waiting on God to show me whatever. After about twenty minutes I started to notice small holes in the clouds and the emergence of the sun behind the cloud covered horizon. A few minutes later while the sun itself was still not visible, small rays of sunshine began to shoot through the holes in the clouds and rest on the ocean's surface like spotlights. They were spectacular and looked like stairways from heaven.

I then noticed something about these beams of light that got me thinking. It was a windy morning and the clouds were moving at a pretty fast pace across the sky. And as they moved the holes in the clouds would move as well and cause these beams of light which were busting through to move across the surface of the ocean as if they were spotlights searching for something or someone! Then, very gently with a soft whisper I heard the Holy Spirit say to me, "What are you thinking?" Immediately my mind went right to one of my favorite verses in scripture, so I opened up my bible to the sixteenth chapter of the book of 2nd Chronicles and read one of my favorite verses, 2nd Chronicles 16:9 which reads, "For the eyes of the Lord range throughout the earth to strengthen those whose hearts are fully committed to him." That's what God wanted to show me this morning at sunrise with those beams of light! That He searches out those on the earth to see whose hearts are fully committed to Him and strengthens them for the journey ahead! God wants my heart fully committed to Him so that I may be able to enjoy, and not throw away, the things He entrusts to me in this life; His very best for me! WOW!!!

So here's the importance of having a committed heart; it allows you to keep the very best of what God desires to give you! Hope allows you to receive God's best, discernment will protect it from the Enemy and a committed heart will allow you to keep it! Living with an uncommitted heart all of my life has caused me to unknowingly push away in fear many of my hearts desires. Gifts such as a wife and family, success and the growth of my companies, the ability to take risks and step out of my comfort zones and most of all to trust my entire life to God and live the adventure He has for me. I want to live life to its fullest and that requires a committed heart! It's time for me to look for the solutions to life's obstacles which will lead me to God's best and not to search for the escape routes that take me away from it. No more escape routes in relationships, no more escape routes in my career; it's time to stop playing safe and start taking wise risks. And finally no more escape routes from God!

I am committing my heart fully to him and going to live the very best life He has for me! It's time to live and not exist! And in order to do so I will have to leave the shoreline, dive into the ocean and swim out far enough that my feet can no longer touch the bottom. It can be scary and unnerving that far out in the ocean, but that's where those who trust God are willing to venture. God also shared with me that morning that most of His children will live their lives on the shoreline getting their feet wet on occasion while playing it safe. But it's not the life He wants for us. He wants us to take a journey with Him filled with adventure and uncertainty. And that will only come once we take the plunge out into the deep waters were faith is our only hope to keep us afloat. It is out there in the middle of the vast ocean and its deep recesses that we will finally hear God call us to the greatest adventure of all, a life lived by faith! He calls to us from the depths of the ocean floor to the depth of our hearts; "**Deep calls to deep** in the roar of your waterfalls; all your waves and breakers have swept over me." Psalm 42:7! But not until we have surrounded ourselves with the depth and the height and the width of God's love can we hear the call and find true faith. I have dived in the ocean and have heard the call, now let the journey continue!

DELIVERANCE FROM FEAR

Another bridge I encountered this year was from 'Fear to Faith'. The one thing different about this bridge was I discovered it when I was already on the bridge of 'Hopesteration'. The lesson I learned from this realization is that God is able to walk us across more than one bridge at a time if He deems it necessary to our growth and restoration. I was made aware of this bridge shortly after the trial God used to deliver me from the fear of man. That trial was the wilderness period of dealing with my fears on the journey from fear to faith. So now I was going to cross the bridge that would lead me to a deeper faith, away from fear and anxiety. The lessons on this bridge began to take shape immediately and I began learning more about truth. Lies as we know are from the wasteland and are spread through fear. Truths are from the garden and grow by faith. If you meditate on lies the results will be stress, anxiety, sickness and disease. If you meditate on truth and the results will be hope, restoration, prosperity and ultimately life!

So what's the key to crossing this bridge? Change your thought life and change your life! What you are thinking directly correlates to how you will live your life and the course it will take. If we are a believer still imprisoned to the wasteland it is because we are thinking and meditating on the lies that have been allowed to take root in our minds and develop strongholds. We also know these strongholds are powerful and impossible to break without God's help. So powerful that if we do not surrender the task of breaking them to God they will keep us chained down as a prisoner to the wasteland our entire life. And that is my greatest fear for my brothers and sisters in Christ; to live in the wasteland apart from God as a believer their entire life! We also don't want to run out ahead of God with our thoughts and end up in the land of Anxiety, which is futuristic thinking apart from God. This type of thinking is filled with worry, which is perverted imagination and a sin against God. So our goal is to get to and remain in the garden which will allow us to live with God in the moment.

So the bridge from 'Fear to Faith' is about the renewing of the mind! Romans 12:2 tells us, "Do not conform to the pattern of this world, but be transformed by the renewing of your mind. Then you will be able to test and approve what God's will is – his good, pleasing and perfect will." There it is folks! Renew (change) your mind, change the way you think and what you meditate on and you will change your life. If we will discipline ourselves to think and meditate on the things of God and not the lies of the Enemy, we will move from a life of fear and anxiety to a life of faith! So as I cross this new bridge I find myself on the front lines of a battle between the pattern of this world and truth; and the battlefield is the mind!

So how does a believer fight this battle? The answer is given in the book of 2nd Corinthians, verses 3-5; "For though we live in the world, we do not wage war as the world does. The weapons we fight with are not the weapons of the world. On the contrary, they have divine power to demolish strongholds. We demolish arguments and every pretension that sets itself up against the knowledge of God, and we take captive every thought to make it obedient to Christ." In order to win the battle of the mind we will have to surrender our natural ability to fight as the world does because the Enemy is just too strong and our chances for victory are slim! But God tells us "The battle is mine says the Lord" and it is His divine power that will demolish the strongholds of the Enemy. Our responsibility in this battle is to take captive every thought that enters our mind and hand it over to 'the obedience of Christ'. In other words, take our thoughts to the cross where

Christ performed His greatest act of obedience; obedience to death that we may live!

Crossing the bridge from 'Fear to Faith' is going to be one of the greatest challenges of my journey to the garden. My consistent thoughts of trying to predict my future has held me captive to anxiety and fear my whole life. One of the greatest benefits of brokenness is the ability to come back to the present from the future in our thinking. Brokenness helps our minds to rest in the moment and leaves the future to God. Faith gives us the courage to live and be led by the Holy Spirit while trusting God with our future. Faith is the courage to walk with God through any danger and go wherever He wants us to go without hesitation! Can't wait to see what next year brings!

SEPARATING SOUL FROM SPIRIT
Year Four

Often in my life I have found myself uttering the phrase "I would be okay with my life if I could get away from my mind!" Why would I say that? What did I mean by that? Those are questions in my mind right now and the very ones I am asking God to answer. I feel as if I have been tortured by my thoughts most of my life. It seems as if I cannot escape my thoughts no matter how hard I try. No matter how bad they would become regarding a variety of topics, I never thought it was possible to change. I just figured I was a slave to my thought life and God would give me a new one when I got to heaven. Romans 7:24 says, "What a wretched man I am! Who is going to rescue me from this body of death? (From this horrible thought life!) Romans 7:25, "Thanks be to God – through Jesus Christ our Lord!" Finally!!! I am about to have my prayer of a changed thought life answered. And it comes through the process of having my soul separated from my spirit.

When I first experienced brokenness back in January of 2010 I discovered that we are triune beings comprised of a spirit, a soul and a body, The Bible tells us we are created in God's image, who is also a triune God; God the Father, God the son Jesus Christ and God the Holy Spirit. It is explained in 1st Thessalonians 5:23, "May God himself, the God of peace, sanctify you through and through. May your whole spirit, soul and body be kept blameless at the coming of our Lord Jesus Christ." Now knowing that we are triune beings and that Gods will is that we be sanctified (to be 'set apart' for a particular use in a special purpose or work and to make holy or sacred), or in other words to become useful to God, I believe we must have our souls restored and separated from our spirits so that God can speak and live through us! Thus invoking us to bring about the Kingdom of God on earth!

So why must we have our soul be separated from our spirit? And what does that look like? These are the questions I believe the Lord is going to address on the next part of my journey to the garden. We now understand that our soul is comprised of our will, mind and emotions, but our spirit is who we truly are, our life force that comes alive when we are born again.

In order for God to use us in the furthering and fulfillment of His kingdom He must have His spirit flow with our spirit through our souls. God's spirit speaks to our spirit (Psalm 42:7) and our spirit is to touch the world with its message. In order for this to happen we must become pure in the sense that our soul does not precede the spirit when God is trying to work through us. God doesn't want our souls, our thoughts, opinions and our emotions to be the first thing the world encounters when they meet us. He wants them to see Jesus first! The Spirit needs a mind, an emotion and a will to express itself. But if a will is not broken it will be the first thing the world around us experiences. Thus a broken and surrendered will (Brokenness) allows God to use us most effectively for bringing about the Kingdom of God here on earth. That is why I believe brokenness is necessary in the life of a believer before God can fully use us as a vessel to reach the world. By the breaking of the will a believer can be conformed to that of God's will and allow God's spirit to flow through.

In this part of my journey I move from Hebrews 4:10-11 to Hebrews 4:12-13. In the first part of my journey I discovered the gift of brokenness and began a journey from the wasteland to the garden by way of the 'Bridge of Brokenness'. The journey was about entering into the rest of God. It was being delivered from the self-will and a lifetime of doing for, rather than resting in, God, which ultimately leads to exhaustion. Hebrews 4:10-11 teaches us, "For anyone who enters God's rest also rests from his own work, just as God did from His. Let us therefore, make every effort to enter that rest, so that no one will fall by following their example of disobedience." These two verses point out the importance of entering God's rest, or moving from the law to Grace.

Entering God's rest is the initial purpose of brokenness. It causes us to cease doing for God and to learn to let God do for us and through us! It is the way God allows us to partake in His Kingdom building. When we enter into God's rest we learn to hear His voice apart from all others and follow Him. Our days of leading our own way are over; we grow up, mature and are then able to be led by the spirit of God. (Romans 8:14) But after we have come to the point in our journey where we now want to experience God's power and have it flow through us like rivers (John 7:38), the separation of soul and spirit must take place. Therefore, we transition to Hebrews 4:12-13,"For the word of God is living and active. Sharper than any doubled edge sword, it penetrates to **dividing even soul and spirit**, joints and marrow; it judges the thoughts and attitudes of the heart. Nothing in all creation is hidden from God's sight. Everything is uncovered and lay bare before the eyes of him to whom we must give account."

So what's happening right now to my soul? I am having my thoughts judged and the attitude of my heart exposed. This is where the teaching from last year that, "God will offend our minds to capture our hearts" begins to bloom! My thought life is under judgment (the act of assessing a situation) in order to expose and purify the motives of my heart! And it was just a week ago in mid-February 2014 while having breakfast with some friends that God began to assess my thought life and start purifying the motives of my heart.

Typically on Friday mornings I will meet with some friends who are all brothers in Christ for breakfast and to have fellowship while discussing almost every topic imaginable. One particular Friday we came across the subject of 'Medical Marijuana' and the use of mind altering drugs. I was the first to address the situation and made my stance very clear; "I am not a proponent of Medical Marijuana or any mind altering drug for any reason whatsoever!" As a former user and dealer of Marijuana I know firsthand its ill effects and the damage it causes not only physically, but mentally and spiritually as well! I know from personal experience the horrible effects that enter into the souls of people who decide to use mind altering drugs. I have suffered almost every one of them and it was not a pleasant experience! So as the discussion grew into a battle with a clear cut divide between accepting and prohibiting the use of mind altering drugs, emotions were intensifying and judgments were being applied; acceptance and grace were lacking, especially on my part! As soon as I was informed that I had offended everyone at the table with my dogmatic point of view, I heard the Holy Spirit say to me as he spoke through one of the other guys, **"It's not**

your opinion that's offending us, it's your delivery!" That statement just stopped me in my tracks and would be a pivotal moment in my life!

'What did he mean by that?' was the thought that went through my mind. I heard it as clear as it could be from my friend's mouth, but I knew it was the Holy Spirit's voice speaking into my heart. I was about to be broken of a very long held belief system that was driven by pride and arrogance! Dogmatism!!! (Definition; the tendency to lay down principles as incontrovertibly true, without consideration of evidence or the opinion of others) "Just because I believe that something is true does not give me the right to force that belief onto others, no matter how convicted I am!" That is lesson number one in the separation of the soul from the spirit; 'Do not attach your worldly thoughts, opinions, beliefs, feelings or personal convictions onto the message God wants to speak through you!' Hence, God must purge our old self (pride) from our new regenerated spirit. This is where the inner man, our old prideful self (old soul) must be purged so that our new soul identified with Christ can flourish. A God given message from our spirit that is tainted by the prideful soul loses its power, the power of God to encourage or transform another. When we attach our prideful soul with its misguided will, judgmental mind and inappropriate emotions to any message that God wants to flow through us to touch this world, the message becomes tainted and has a greater ability to offend! (Proverbs 18:19) "An offended brother is more unyielding than a fortified city and disputes are like the barred gates of a citadel"

When people encounter our flesh instead of our spirit, they get offended. God wants to use those who belong to Him to guide others over bridges on their journeys and not for us to build walls that will hinder them along the way. That's what broken people do; they allow God to build bridges and help others walk across them. Broken people are 'bridge guides' to help others on their journey from the wasteland to the garden. Broken people are safe people!

One of the major reasons why we must have our souls separated from our spirits is so that we can become safe people. This is what I believe God has in mind for those who want to be of service to Him in the building of his kingdom. We cannot be useful instruments in the hand of God if our flesh is tainting our inner man, our soul and our spirit. When we have this mixture of flesh and spirit we can come across as a beacon of light and a cause of pain at the same time. I know I am guilty of this at times. I have also experienced this far too many times with believers I have walked with or encountered along my journey. The intent is always one of encouragement for the heart of someone hurting, but the result can be a stab wound to the heart if the message is not coming from a pure heart with pure motives. So my prayer is, "Lord make me a safe person; one who helps to heal wounds and not cause them."

I now can see how the breaking of my will and the discovery of hope were necessary to come this far in my journey. It is a beautiful picture of the Lord restoring my soul step by step. First my will is broken and conformed to His, and then I am introduced to hope, which is necessary for the renewing of the mind. That is a major part of separating the soul from the spirit, renewing the mind (Romans 12:2). God has given me the mind of Christ (Romans 15:5) and has placed a helmet on my head and my mind called the 'hope of salvation'. It is now my responsibility to train my mind to hope; to have a confident expectation of good always. Discovering hope last year and stepping on to the bridge from a 'Wasteland Pessimist' to a 'Garden Optimist' were prerequisites to the separation of my soul and spirit. Safe people have hope, they are optimists and they are broken souls wanting to help heal the brokenhearted souls they encounter! (Titus 2:11-14)

HURTING PEOPLE HURT PEOPLE

Over the past few months the Lord has been preparing me and teaching me on the second half of brokenness which I believe is the separating of the soul and spirit. He exposed it to me through a conversation I had with some friends in which I came across as very dogmatic and opinionated, as well as unwilling to accept their view on the topic. It was pointed out to me that it wasn't my opinion that bothered them but my delivery that offended them. What the Lord is revealing to me is that the Kingdom of God is not about black and white thinking or opinions (dogmatism); it's about love! It's about leaving judgement behind so acceptance can bloom!

I learned a huge lesson about acceptance and myself one night. Let me set the stage and explain how the Lord opened my eyes. I was watching a mixed martial arts fight and on this particular night there was a semifinal fight between two fighters. One of the fighters was a bit older; very talented, well-spoken and polished "That's my guy!" was my initial thought. The other fighter was also very talented, but younger and a bit more abrasive, self-confident, talkative and not quite as polished or politically astute as his opponent. He came across as cocky, immature and not initially likable as his picture perfect teammate.

So here we go; the opponents are in their corners and the bell is about to ring. The older fighter with his well-stocked corner of coaches and teammates, plus the vast majority of the other fighters ready to cheer for him vs. the other younger guy all alone in his corner. They come out swinging and battle through the first round and I give a slight edge to the older fighter. The second round is in play and going somewhat just like the first round until all of a sudden, BAM!!! The older fighter throws a roundhouse right punch that lands on the jaw of his opponent and all you heard was, CRACK!!! The dude drops to his knees immediately and is out, broken jaw and the fight is over; didn't really see that coming but it happened. The room went silent and everybody was just looking on in awe of what just happened, except for the older fighter who was elated and couldn't contain himself. After helping the wounded fighter up they came to the center of the ring and the referee declared the older fighter the winner by knockout. It was hard to watch and my heart just went out to this poor young kid who was devastated and severely hurt. He could barely speak as blood poured from his mouth. But what happened next would change my life forever!

After the fight was over the camera found this wounded kid just sitting in a chair in a corner of the gym by himself crying as one of his teammates walks over to console him. They spoke for a little bit as the defeated fighter made it known to his teammate that he felt no one had his back, even this particular teammate himself wouldn't sit in his corner. This was a teammate that wanted to remain neutral because he was friends with both fighters. Then the camera zoomed in on the wounded fighter and I will never forget the words he spoke as he was crying, "This hurts so bad, I can get over the broken jaw, but the betrayal and abandonment I'll never forget! Everybody left me, I was all alone! That's what really hurts!" Hearing those words rocked me and I went to bed feeling like I somehow played a part in what just happened on the TV.

I awoke the next morning to have my quiet time and was in the middle of praying and giving thanks to God to start my day when my mind started to wander. It eventually came back to the scene of the fighter sitting in the corner and his cry for help and desire to be understood. The Holy Spirit began to ask me questions which were piercing straight into my heart. "Who do you think represented the kingdom of God with his actions, the self-confident winner or the wounded soul?" Wow!!! Proverbs 20:11 again came to my mind, "Even a child is known by actions (*not his words*), by whether his conduct is pure and right." This brought me back to last year's lesson, "Don't listen to what people say; watch how they live their life!" So God used the imagery of two different fighters to speak to me and teach me a very important lesson.

All I could hear in my mind were the questions, "How many times have you done this same thing? When will it stop? How many more people do you need to punch in their mouths who disagree with your opinion? Do you have to be right while others are wrong? Does everything still have to be black and white? Could you both be right, or both wrong? How many more moves do you need to make in order to stack the odds in your favor? How far are you going to retreat into your safe little world in order to avoid those who are wounded and can hurt you? Before I could even begin to start answering these questions I fell on my knees and began to weep like a child. I was crushed by the weight of God's love for me to finally open the door to this prison of a dogmatic existence. I knew immediately that I was going to start opening my eyes to living life in such a way where loves covers all offenses. No longer was I going to try and survive on my own in this fallen world. My pride in being a survivor was just struck a death blow. I remember thinking it is now time to thrive and not just survive in my safe little world where no one can challenge me!

You see, God showed me through that mixed martial arts fight that I can be that self-confident self-reliant fighter. I often was the bible quoting believer going around punching everyone in the mouth that disagreed with my opinion. Even if they were hurting and crying out for help, I wasn't going to risk losing anything I held dear to me such as my beliefs, convictions, opinions, attitudes and my faith. I just wasn't going to lay anything down that I felt I could lose, I wasn't prepared to lay my life down for Jesus or anyone else! But this experience taught me one of life's greatest lessons, "It's okay to lay your life down for Jesus and others because you only keep what you give away!" It's time to let go because only a fool holds on to things that will kill him.

A fool is also referred to as a 'mocker' in the bible. So this morning God gave me a verse to further separate my worldly focused soul from my Christ focused spirit, Proverbs 22:10 says, "Drive out the mocker, and out goes strife; quarrels and insults are ended." My days of mocking everything in this world that I disagree with are coming to an end, it's time to start loving and stop mocking!

So part of God's work to separate my soul from my spirit is to drive out the mocker in me! It's that part of my flesh that tells me everything is either my way or the highway, and that there can be no ground for honest disagreement and compromise. It says only one person can be right and all who disagree with them are wrong. That is the way an immature little child thinks. And when this child grows up he has a tendency to try and punch everyone in the mouth who disagrees with him and if he does his job well enough they can end up with a broken jaw. I am speaking figuratively here of course!

So what do I mean by punching people in the mouth who disagree with my opinions and beliefs? It could mean the silent treatment, so as to say their opinion does not even register with me. It could mean a facial expression that shows my disgust with their thinking. It could mean raising my voice to the point of calling them out in order to silence their view. It could mean insulting them in some way so as to make it personal, might even be a back door insult. It could be the use of sarcasm, which translates to 'one who tears the flesh' (stab wound). Or better yet, the queen mother of them all, I could quote scripture to prove my point beyond question! What have I been thinking?!!! This isn't bridge building with love; it is the building of walls to prevent love from doing its work.

Think about that verse from Proverbs 22:10 for a minute! Once the mocker in you is gone, the strife of life and the meaningless quarrels we have that are filled with insults towards one another are driven out as well. I am sitting here salivating for the day this mocker in me is cast into the ocean to drown and never return. I am so tired of this mocker robbing me of relationships for the sake of having to be right, even if it's only in my eyes. And let me be honest with you, I have the perfect justification for this mocker in me; I'm from Jersey! I am serious! I have used that excuse all my life. I can be brash, boastful, arrogant, hard, impatient, always right and never apologizing. It's a Jersey thing right! No it is not, it's the flesh! My lifelong excuse just ran out; what am I going to do? How about grow up!

So I am sensing a new bridge here and it feels somewhat like one from a 'Mocker' to a 'Lover'. Galatians 5:14-15 says, "The entire law is fulfilled in keeping this one command: "Love your neighbor as yourself." But if you bite and devour each other, watch out or you will be destroyed by each other." That's what mockers do, they destroy others by biting and beating them with their flesh till the other person is destroyed. I think it's time to muster up the courage to step onto this new bridge from 'A Mocker to a Lover'. This one should be a doozy!

MOCKER TO LOVER

I just entered a new season on my journey to become 'A Childlike Man'. It is a new bridge that I must cross called from "A Mocker to a Lover". This is going to be a tough bridge because I have lived with the mocker in me for my entire life. I am so intertwined with him it is hard to tell us apart at times and that's not good! God says the entire law of life can be summed up in a single command: (Galatians 5:14) "Love your neighbor as yourself." And then the Lord warns us about disobeying this command; (Galatians 5:15) "If you keep on biting and devouring each other, watch out or you will be destroyed by each other." I will be the first to admit that I have seen the mocker in me destroy way too many people in my life who simply disagreed with me or posed some sort of perceived threat to my safe little world. I sit here today with all of the sincerity I can muster and say to God, "Please drive that mocker out of me!" I am so sick and tired of living in strife over petty disagreements that result in quarrels and personal insults towards others. I am so sick and tired of having to be right and prove everyone else wrong. The mocker must go so that the lover in me, the Spirit of God, can flow freely through me.

The bible explains why mockers are the way they are and what motivates them. Proverbs 21:24 says, "The proud and arrogant person- "Mocker" is his name- behaves with insolent fury." Mockers do what they do out of arrogance and pride. When a person is prideful they get all puffed up, but their puffiness comes from air which means there is no substance to them. That's why they mock others; fear of exposure to what they really are, empty. They have to mock others to lift themselves up. Most people do not like mockers because they are irritating and destructive, full of criticism and cynicism. 1st Corinthians 8:1-2 says it well, "Knowledge puffs up, but love builds up."

This bridge is such an important part of the continuation of learning to walk with God (Walking in the Spirit) which was a lesson I learned last year and the new lesson of the separation of the soul and the spirit. If we will learn to hear God's voice and walk with Him on our journey, hence 'Walking in the Spirit', the acts of our flesh (The Mocker) will not be able to manifest in us because they cannot coexist. Galatians 5:13-26 says:

"You, my brothers and sisters, were called to be free. But do not use your freedom to indulge the flesh; rather, serve one another humbly in love. For the entire law is fulfilled in keeping this one command: "Love your neighbor as yourself." If you bite and devour each other, watch out or you will be destroyed by each other. So I say, walk by the Spirit, and you will not gratify the desires of the flesh. For the flesh desires what is contrary to the Spirit and the Spirit what is contrary to the flesh. They are in conflict with each other, so that you are not to do whatever you want. But if you are led by the Spirit, you are not under the law. The acts of the flesh are obvious: sexual immorality, impurity and debauchery; idolatry and witchcraft; hatred, discord, jealousy, fits of rage, selfish ambition, dissensions, factions and envy; drunkenness, orgies, and the like. I warn you, as I did before, that those who live like this will not inherit the kingdom of God. But the fruit of the Spirit is love, joy, peace, forbearance, kindness, goodness, faithfulness, gentleness and self-control. Against such things there is no law. Those who belong to Christ Jesus have crucified the flesh with its passions and desires. Since we live by the Spirit, let us keep in step with the Spirit. Let us not become conceited, provoking and envying each other."

Once again I cannot say it better than the scriptures themselves. What the Father is saying to me is the 'Mocker' cannot coexist with the 'Spirit of God'. They war against one another and the result is conflict in our soul which manifests itself as conflict in our lives! As stated above in the scriptures, the mocker consists of the 'Acts of the Flesh'. When we are living by our flesh instead of by the spirit, we will naturally perform the acts of the flesh in our day to day life. We will be okay with sexual immorality and the acts of fornication and adultery. We will have no problem getting drunk and living in debauchery. We will have no problem chasing idols such as money, power and status above the pursuit of God himself. We will have no problem dabbling in the occult, in such things as horoscopes, new age mysticism and drugs. We will have no problem living with a dogmatic world view which causes hatred, discord, jealousy, fits of rage, selfish ambition, dissensions, factions, quarrels and all sorts of strife! That is why God warns us so many times in the bible about this mocker or fool, and the acts he performs in and through our flesh. God says the one who lives like this will not inherit the kingdom of God.

What is the kingdom of God? The fruit of the Spirit! The kingdom of God is found in the garden as we rest in God's love for us. That is why God refers to good character as "the fruit of the spirit". Fruit grows from healthy trees that are planted in gardens whose leaves are always green and bear fruit in every season of life! The mocker is not allowed in the garden because his acts of the flesh would kill and destroy every piece of fruit that is being produced. The mocker is full of weeds (Lies) and driven by fear. Remember Adam and Eve. The moment they disobeyed God and became fools and mockers and started to blame one another as well as lie about their actions, God drove them out of the garden. Strife, quarrels and insults were now staples of their life and God would have no part of it in paradise, His garden! And to this day God has cherubim angels and flaming swords blocking the entrance to the Garden of Eden so that no mocker may enter and destroy the fruit growing within the garden! (Genesis 3:23) We will talk more about this bridge later as I journey across it.

ISLAND OF SELF-LOVE

So I asked God the questions; where does the bridge from 'A Mocker to a Lover' take you from and lead you to? And what's its ultimate purpose? With a smile God said to me, "I am going to show you in a huge way, the best way I know how, and that is through experience!" You see, the one thing I have learned in the past several years is that you may know something to be true in your mind, but until you experience it in your heart through life's circumstances, you can't really possess it! You need experience to make truth real in your life!

So as you know over the past seven months I have been spending my time between Atlanta and Wrightsville Beach NC. My time here on the island of Wrightsville Beach has consisted of some serious alone time, either watching sunrises on the ocean horizon in the morning, a sunset into Banks Channel in the evening, or sitting next to a fire between the two bodies of water while chilling out and quietly listening to God. All together it has been a serious time of isolation consisting of deep introspective thoughts, but also the quietness and stillness needed to go much deeper in my relationship with God. So now it is mid-April and I really started to ponder why I was compelled over the past several years and especially this past one to move away from Atlanta and head to this tiny, somewhat remote island which is two bridges away from the mainland.

After having a couple of discussions with some of my mentors, the same ones who helped me see that God was taking me away from Atlanta for a season, the clouds finally opened up and I could hear Him say," I am taking you off of the island of self-love and out of the prison you have been in since you were three years old! The time of loving yourself more than others is over. I am taking you to Relationshipville!" I will have to admit that I was stunned! I hit the floor on my knees with such mixed emotions. What have I been doing? Why now? Why not twenty years ago? What did I do wrong? How did I end up here? This is the greatest news of my life! Is it too late for relationship? Can it all be restored? So you were listening to my cries all these years! Then I just simply looked up and said, "Thank you Papa!"

I said it because it was the first time I think I have ever really felt love in my heart. I know that sounds harsh, or sad, or pitiful, or desperate or painful, or maybe all of the above. But it was true; I had finally come to the realization that I am loved by God. I had always known it to be true, but now I believed it in my heart. I have the experience to make it real in my life! I couldn't explain the feeling, but God then began to immediately give me insight to the purpose of my being here alone on an island for the past seven months.

It all started to make more sense as I began to receive answers to the many questions that had rattled around in my mind the past year and a half. God revealed to me the length, depth and height to His purposes in every move He had made to get me here. Think about it. In that period of time, I had sold the house I lived in for the past 12 years and said goodbye to some of the best neighbors in the world. I had my business cut in half and suffered an eighty percent decrease in my income. I ended up moving into my friend's basement apartment for six months waiting to hear from God to direct the next steps of my life. Then finally I heard the call to pack up and leave Atlanta because I was 'root bound' and needed to grow.

I said goodbye to friends and people that I had lived and walked with through many hills and valleys over the past twenty five years. I left all my comforts, safety nets and security blankets behind and moved seven hours away to an island two bridges away from my nearest friends; Talk about isolation! Not only that, but I was going to try and be a custom clothier of men's fine suits at the beach where most people wear shorts, t-shirts and flip flops! Why go to such an extreme to teach me a lesson? I will tell you.

In His amazing love for me, God knew the best way for me to understand what He was doing in me spiritually, was to have me experience it physically. He knew I had come to the end of my rope with being alone in this world and that it would become detrimental to my life's purpose for the Kingdom if I were to remain alone on the island of self-love much longer. That's why He had a friend share with me the phrase 'root bound'. Sometimes you have to actually be physically removed from somewhere and re-planted before you turn in on yourself and die. I was dying on the island of self-love. One of the first things I started to notice when I was alone at the beach was that I really hated being alone and in isolation. What made it worse were the incredible views. It should have seemed like paradise, but it wasn't. Having the perfect environment actually exposed the aloneness more. I kept thinking to myself, this is beautiful, but it is empty!

Life and all its beauty doesn't add up to much without relationship. I have heard it said before that a man's wealth is predicated upon the depths of his relationships; during this time I felt broke! So as I sat every morning watching the sun rise off the ocean and then sit every night and watch it set in the bay, I began to feel the heaviness of self-love and the despair of loneliness it brought. You see, it knew it's time in me was coming to an end and it began to fight for its survival. I then started to ask myself questions like; have I ever really been in love? Or, have I ever loved anyone else more than I loved myself? I don't know! It was a devastating conclusion to come to, but the exact one needed to point me in the direction of the bridge that was soon to get me off this island of self-love.

This is when I began dealing with the 'mocker' within. Mockers are so self-absorbed that they tend to push people away from them before they can get hurt. It is a self-protection strategy that if mastered will eventually lead us to a life lived alone in a prison on the island of self-love. Unfortunately I had mastered it! And as I previously stated, the mocker in me was skilled at the arts of silent treatments, eye rolling, raising my voice, sarcasm and bible quoting. And with these tools of the mocker there is only one possible thing you can construct; a wall!

There is no bridge building going on in the life of a mocker. That is why God opened my eyes to Proverbs 22:10 "Drive out the mocker and out goes strife…" And the walls come down too! That's one thing the mocker doesn't realize is that when he pushes people away with self-protection and mocks those who try to help, what eventually happens is that he ends up building walls in life from the inside out. And when the job is completely finished and the walls are erected, he realizes he has built himself his own personal prison where no one can enter and hurt him, but where he can't escape either! That's the deceit of the mocker; he turns you into your own worst enemy. There is very little chance of you getting out of your own way; after all, you are trapped in a self-contained prison of self!

So little by little I had begun to piece together that this entire situation in which I found myself was a perfectly constructed circumstance hand crafted by God to take me physically to the place I had been living in my soul. God knew if He could get me to experience in the physical realm what was happening in the spiritual realm the pain of the experience would be so powerful as to cause me to disregard everything the mocker had ever taught me and step on to the bridge from 'A mocker to a lover' in record speed. It worked!

Shortly after he revealed to me His purpose of sending me to this island for a season of my life, God gave me a song to listen to over and over whose lyrics just rocked me! I heard it on the radio and then couldn't get it out of my head. I then realized after I looked up its lyrics that I myself must have written it. The words summed up the futility of my life on the Island of Self-Love. They echoed my pain and the constant prayers I threw up to

God over and over again as I struggled to find life in the prison of self. They described the constant barrage of so many people pointing out my faults giving me the sense that I was crazy or had issues beyond repair and I just wasn't getting it; the culmination of all that left me believing that there was something wrong with me! But I understand all that because to the natural eye a broken soul looks broke and in need of fixing. But in truth, a broken soul isn't broke it is surrendered. "Broken souls don't need to be fixed, they need to be loved! That's because they are not used to living in love!" Broken souls are desperate for love!

Broken souls who are about to be set free from the prison of self and released from the island of self-love desperately need God and His love. They have finally come to the realization they are not in control but that God is. It looks messy and it's meant to be that way. Life is messy and so are relationships. Broken people are learning to live in that mess, but the natural world sees them differently and treats them like fixer-upper projects. That's why unbroken people are always trying to fix broken people. It looks scary to them and they feel the need to step in and straighten it all out. To them it looks like that person's world is falling apart, but that's just it! God is dismantling the old self so that Christ might rebuild it and reign in them. Broken people don't need fixing; they need love and acceptance because they aren't accustomed to having that in their life. After all, they have been alone in a prison on an isolated island their entire life. They have been unable to give or receive love unconditionally due to the many walls and barriers of protection they've erected.

You likely have heard of the song 'Somebody to Love' by Queen. It was written and sung by lead singer Freddy Mercury. I believe Freddy as expressed in the song's lyrics had the same longing to be set free from the prison of self like I did. Just ponder the following line: **"I just gotta get out of this prison cell, Someday I'm gonna be free, Lord!"**

But there is way out of the prison of self-life; brokenness! And again, it is a gift from God to be embraced, not an invitation to be fixed! So now as I begin crossing the bridge from 'A Mocker to a Lover', I take my first steps knowing that God loves me and is not disappointed in me. I am learning to live life as a loved person! That's where the journey on this bridge begins, believing that God really does love us! You see, until we have the experience and belief that God truly does love us, we are incapable of giving or receiving love from others

BACK TO ATLANTA

I discovered that my time on Wrightsville Beach Island was temporary and the Lord was going to bring me back to Atlanta on April 27th 2014. I began my day in quiet time and was talking to the Lord about a fear of mine that I wanted removed from my thought life. It was the fear of loss! Again, knowing that fears come from believing a lie about God, I realized I had bought the lie early on in life that if I wasn't perfect God would take everything away from me. I remember hearing the phrase "You are not going to learn anything till I take everything away from you" hundreds of times as a child. It was the threat I was given many times when I was being scolded. It just stuck with me! So what I learned to do from this threat was live life with tightly clenched fists. Knowing that I wasn't perfect and could lose everything in an instant taught me to be a perfectionist and hold on tightly to all I believed and possessed in life; it was my only hope; but a false hope at that!

God knew that my strength to hold on tightly to life was fading. I didn't have the ability to carry the load of life on my own anymore, and this lie was going to have to be uprooted. At 7:00 a.m. that morning as I was in my quiet time and wrote this in my journal; "I still need to totally open my hands for what God has for my life. They are not used to being open. Now I must learn to receive! Holy Spirit teach me!" Then I proceeded to write what I felt the Holy Spirit spoke back to me; "Give me your hands (clenched fists) and let's throw them into the sea. It will teach you to live with open arms and open hands. I will teach you to receive!" That was the journaling of my quiet time conversation with the Lord on the morning of April 27th as I sat and stared at the ocean out my window. Later that afternoon as I went out back to watch the sunset, I decided to open the Jesus Calling app in my phone and read it as I prepared for the sun to set on Banks Channel. Here's what I read;

Jesus Calling April 27… "COME TO ME with empty hands and an open heart, ready to receive abundant blessings. I know the depth and breadth of your neediness. Your life-path has been difficult, draining you of strength. Come to Me for nurture. Let Me fill you up with My Presence: I in you, and you in Me. My Power flows most freely into weak ones aware of their need for Me. Faltering steps of dependence are not lack of faith; they are links to My Presence."

I do not believe in coincidences! Having that time of isolation on the Island enabled me to hear Gods voice so clearly at times, as well as having no chance to miss His confirmations. I just knew in my heart at that moment that I was going to say goodbye to the Island of Self-Love in a few months and head back to Atlanta with open hands, open arms and an open heart ready to receive whatever God felt was best for my life. I felt a huge sense of relief at that moment, but it was also followed by a bit of anxiety, because I then realized I had never lived that way before and would have a huge task ahead of me when I got back. But no matter what fears tried to creep into the next part of my journey as I headed back to Atlanta, my new found hope that I discovered earlier would drown them out.

I had a confident expectation that good was on its way. So come June 1st I packed up my car, rolled out of the driveway and quietly said goodbye to the Island of Self-Love as I crossed over the two small bridges headed to the mainland. I drove quite a few miles that trip with my knees on the steering wheel as I opened my hands and arms wide, while praying and thanking God for this amazing journey. I was excited to get home but did not have a clue what would be in store for me when I got there. I just knew that my life would never be the same.

MOCKERS QUESTION BUT LOVERS ASK

Though my transition back to Atlanta seemed smooth at first, it wasn't long before I found myself in the middle of my first spiritual battle. Maybe I thought I would be left alone for a while to settle in the next phase of my journey, but that was naïve. Two weeks in to my return I would experience what I felt to be oppression and resistance from many angles, especially my work. For some reason after having one of my businesses close and a turnover in my bookkeeping personnel, I seemed to have a great deal of strife and miscommunication with all my accounting and personal help. On several occasions where I tried to extract information from those in charge of my accounting and bookkeeping, I felt resistance and conflict build up between myself and those working for me. So much so, that each and every person I had helping me run my business had threatened to quit or resign. And it wasn't really that bad of a situation, it just seemed to escalate every time I tried to get information from one of them.

So I went to the Lord in prayer and asked Him for wisdom and discernment concerning my situation. Now of course, the mocker in me wanted to go to war and fire everyone who was challenging me and my authority as the business owner. I felt I had a right to ask the questions I was asking and deserved to be given a straight forward and truthful answer. After all, I am the one writing the checks. Is that too much to ask? No! But the Holy Spirit made it really clear to me; it's not what you are asking for, it's the way you are asking for it! Sound familiar?

That's when I realized I was getting my next lesson on the bridge from 'A Mocker to a Lover"; the mocker questions people, but a lover asks questions! It was parallel to the first lesson I learned on this bridge; it's not your opinion that offends us, it's how you deliver it! Have to admit it; I had no idea that something of that nature could cause so much strife. How many times in my life have I said, "I don't understand why you are getting upset, all I am doing is asking you a question!" And little did I know that it was not the question I was asking, it was the way I asked it and the tone in which I asked. A mocker will always come from an angle of mistrust and will have an accusatory tone with his questions because he doesn't trust anyone. The mocker also has a predetermined answer he wants in return to his question because he already thinks he knows the truth. He is not asking for information, he is questioning for a confession! This too is part of the mockers dogmatic thinking.

He either believes he is always right and therefore asks questions in such a manner as to expose anyone who disagrees with him, that way he can determine if this particular person is a threat or not, or his continued questioning is really his quest for a different answer than the one he was given because he simply doesn't trust the person he is questioning. God knows that relationships are built on trust but the mocker is not capable of trusting anyone who doesn't agree with him one hundred percent of the time.

Wow!!! I don't know what to say, but again, thank you Papa! What another amazing lesson in my journey from a mocker to a lover, and a few more steps away from the Island of Self-Love. Lovers ask questions because they truly care about people and the situations they may be facing. They ask questions so they can truly get to know another person. Lovers ask questions to make others feel accepted, not exposed! Their questions are meant to gather more information about the other person so they may know how to love them that much more. A friend of mine would always tell me that when I go out on a date I should be a question asking machine. I now understand what that means. My days of interrogating women to find their hidden faults and avoid potential disaster are over. Sorry ladies, I just didn't know!

BEING ESTABLISHED

Here is the next thing I heard from God when I got back to Atlanta, "I am now going to establish you!" This came about while I was having a conversation with a friend. We were discussing my transition back to Atlanta to possibly settle down once and for all, when he made the comment, "you know, there is something to be said about establishment!" I am not sure what he believed he was referring to by 'establishment', but I took it as an establishment of my life and living situation. In other words, I was finally going to settle down in my career, possibly with a family of my own, a new house and all other aspects of an established life. But it sure wasn't what God was talking about. He was talking about the true kind of establishment that brings the true blessings in life. He was going to establish me "In Righteousness!" Wow, was I fooled! I had taken what my friend said and just ran with it in my mind. It rocked me at first until God began to slowly reveal to me that being established in righteousness first was paramount to being able to receive His blessings; as the bible says in Matthew 6:33, "But seek first His kingdom and His righteousness, and all these things will be given to you as well."

What I have come to believe is that when we finally realize that God loves us perfectly because of what Jesus did on the cross on our behalf we can then truly begin to enjoy life! That is what God meant by telling me He is going to establish me. I was going to be established in His righteousness and love! You see, ever since I was young (3 years old!) I have been afraid. There, I said it! For whatever reason, for all my life I have felt that if was not perfect I was going to be punished and for that reason I have lived my whole life in fear. I have been on a quest to reach the point of perfection so I could finally enjoy life and not be driven by the fear of punishment.

But I am done! I quit! I'll never make it! And thank God for that. The days of trying to measure up for God are over. I have come to the end of my own righteousness and now will be established in the righteousness of Jesus Christ. In Paul's letter to the Philippians he writes in chapter 3 verses 8-9,"… that I may gain Christ and be found in Him, not having a righteousness of my own that comes from the law, but that which is through faith in Christ – the righteousness that comes from God and is by faith." The reason I believe I am able to finally hear God speak to me about righteousness is because I am beginning to believe that God truly loves me. That's what happened earlier this year while I was living on Wrightsville beach. I came to the realization that God loves me perfectly and will do anything it takes for me to realize that.

And what does Love do best? It drives out fear! That is exactly what the Apostle tells us in the first letter of John. In chapter 4 verse 18 he says, "There is no fear in love. But perfect love drives out fear, because fear has to do with punishment. The one who fears is not made perfect in love." That is such a beautiful promise. First God reveals to me that He is driving out the 'mocker' in me (Proverbs 22:10), and now it is revealed to me that His perfect love is driving the fear out of me. That is a double portion of blessing that just consumes my heart. The more God drives out the mockery and fear, the more room for His love to fill me!

I am beginning to understand just how important being established in the righteousness of Christ is for the believer. It delivers us from all of our worries, fears and attempts to get right with God by our own performance. Being established in righteousness lets us know the true meaning of Jesus' last words, "It is finished." (TETELESTAI) Everything that needed to be done for us to be right with God (become righteous) was finished at the cross. There is nothing left for us to do but receive from God and enjoy his endless love and blessings! This is the end of perfectionism because I am perfectly loved from a Perfect Father because of His perfect Son's sacrifice.

This is such a huge revelation for me on my journey. I don't believe I could have gone any further in my faith unless I went through the last 18 months of wondering in the dessert. God knew exactly what needed to be done in order for my eyes to be opened to His love and my righteousness in His son Jesus. Now I know the true meaning of 'Root-bound'. I had grown as much as I could grow in the pot that I was in. I needed to be up-rooted and temporarily moved so that God could prepare a new larger pot for me to be established in and grow to my full potential. What an amazing God!

FROM THINKING TO BELIEVING

So as I pondered this process of being repotted a new bridge was laid before me and it lead from 'Thinking like Lot' to 'Believing like Abraham'. Both of these men were righteous, meaning they were right with God. Peter called Lot righteous in the New Testament and it was recorded in Genesis 15 that, "Abraham believed the Lord, and He credited it to him as righteousness." But there are stark contrasts to these two men. Lot was a drifter who tended to find himself in many precarious situations. He lacked focus and purpose and when confronted with choices his first reaction was always to think of himself. Abraham on the other hand typically tried to avoid conflicts but when pressed into them he allowed his opponents to set the rules for settling the dispute. Lot drifted through life and it eventually cost him all he had. Abraham walked with purpose and believed God when He said, "Go, walk through the length and breathe of the land, for I am giving it to you."

Thinking like Lot leads to self-absorption and will take you to places in life you don't want to be. As difficult as it may be to walk in the unknown and trust God, believing like Abraham will lead you to the best possible life. Not the easiest, the best! What this bridge tells me is to stop trying to think my way through life and start living by faith and walking in the unknown. Abraham walked through his fears. He wasn't always truthful, he lied out of fear, but he kept on walking. He believed and obeyed God for the direction and purpose of his life, even when he didn't understand.

So what happens when we cross this bridge of righteousness, from thinking to believing? We receive a promise from God, one that I have waited all of my life to receive. It is found in the Old Testament in a book called Isaiah, chapter 54 verse 14, "In righteousness you will be established: Tyranny will be far from you; you will have nothing to fear. Terror will be far removed; it will not come near you." That is a promise I receive with opens arms and an open heart. For someone who has been afraid all his life there could not be a more comforting promise than that. Once we are established in righteousness the Enemy no longer can imprison us with fear. I don't know about you but I am sick and tired of fear based living. I want out and God's perfect love is the solution.

NAKED TURTLE

I want to share with you how I was able to make it through the barrage of doubt and fear that consumed me when I returned to Atlanta. After I heard the words, "I am going to establish you", I immediately tried to help God out by anticipating this establishment and positioning myself to receive it the way I thought best. All that did was sink me into a valley of darkness and despair. God wasn't going to let me interfere with the perfect work He was doing inside of me. That's what self-righteous people do, they perform and position outwardly which ultimately will hinder what God is doing inwardly. So God began to teach me some important principles to help me get through this time of transition.

The first principle He taught me was to 'rest in transition'. We have learned on the first part of the journey that rest requires that we cease from our own works. It is not our responsibility to get ourselves through this transition, it is God's. As a matter of fact our growth is always the work of God in us. We are God's workmanship! So what does it mean to 'rest in transition?' It means just that; rest, stop striving to do and listen to the voice of God while in a time of transition. And why is that so important?

I have noticed that some of the most painful mistakes we make in life are when we jump out ahead of God during a time of waiting and transitioning. I see it all the time. We tend to let fear get the best of us in a time of transition because we feel as if we are being left behind or have been totally forgotten by God. Someone loses a job and immediately panics as if God won't provide so they chase after a new one and jump into a situation that is not good and not where God wants them. Someone else gets divorced and immediately tries to fill the void of loneliness thinking God has abandoned them and ends up in a relationship much more destructive than the previous one. There are many ways we can shipwreck the plan of God for our life during transition because it can be a time of loneliness and vulnerability and the Enemy looks to devour those who are feeling lonely and vulnerable.

Now I do believe that there needs to be a shipwreck during a transition period and I call it "crashing the ship of loneliness!" I heard it once said that 'Jesus isn't enough till He's all you have.' Maybe that is what God is doing in us when we go through a time of transition and are feeling lonely, abandoned and vulnerable; He is helping us to know and believe that we have everything we need in Christ, including our righteousness. The way I see it is I have paddled the ship of my own righteousness out in the sea of life for far too long. I have finally run out of my own strength and can paddle no more! Think about the prophet Elijah for a moment. He was one of God's most famous and dramatic prophets. He helped slay the priests of Baal and restored a dead child back to life. Elijah also chose to do life and ministry alone and often paid for it with isolation and loneliness.

But it was in those times of isolation that Elijah was able to hear God very clearly for direction in his life. It wasn't during the storm, earthquake or fire that Elijah heard God, it was a gentle whisper that spoke to him. Elijah learned to hear God while at rest. So therefore I have tossed the paddles and am allowing my 'do it yourself ship of loneliness' to crash upon the shore so I can walk up on the beach, pull up a chair, and rest. Therefore I believe it is imperative that we learn to rest, relax, take a step back, be still and trust God during a time of transition. The second principle God taught me to get through a time of transition was to learn to, 'Sit in the uncomfortable!' I was taught this principle through the story of a 'naked turtle!' There once was a turtle that lost its shell and scurried around frantically looking for it. Eventually the turtle found itself in a briar patch trapped at every side by extremely sharp thorns. Each and every movement that turtle made would be met with the prick or scratch of a painful thorn that would ultimately leave a scar. It was in a vulnerable situation. The turtle's only hope was to rest, relax, be still and trust that it would eventually be set free. That naked turtle had to learn to sit in the uncomfortable till it was rescued and set back in its shell. Most likely a bigger and better shell!

That's what it can feel like as well in a time of transition; uncomfortable!

But learning to sit in the uncomfortable can teach us many lessons. It helps us to realize that we live in a broken, fallen world that truly feels like a wasteland with many pitfalls and briar patches looking to enslave us. It can teach us that for now life here on earth won't be a picnic every day. That there will be many uncomfortable situations and circumstances along our life journeys and we will have to deal with them, or better yet learn to trust God to see us through them.

One of the great lessons I am learning sitting here in my own uncomfortable right now is that when I sit and rest, God works! I sense that I am not interfering with God's work in my life when I sit in the uncomfortable and trust that He is working on my behalf. I am realizing that I am better able to receive all God has for me when I let go of 'doing' and start 'being'. I'm finding that resting and sitting in the uncomfortable also means coming out of it with less pricks, scratches and scars from the briars. I don't know about you but I feel as if I have enough scars from running ahead of God to last several lifetimes. And when it comes to obtaining these scars I am truly realizing that 'less is more!' So I sit, and I wait, and I trust and believe that God knows where I am and He knows where I'm going, even if it is uncomfortable at the moment.

OPEN THE EYES OF MY HEART

What an amazing year this has been. It started out with God addressing my thought life and a promise that to renew it would change my life. Little did I know that the Enemy had taken root in so many areas of my mind? My mind seemed like a prison and the Enemy was the warden with a vow never to let me escape. An even bigger surprise was the introduction to my cell mate 'the Mocker'. Wow! Where did he come from? Who let him into my mind? Will he ever leave? Is it possible to undo all his damage? Can I ever recover? These questions were addressed by my perfect heavenly Father in ways I could never have imagined. Seriously! In order to have my mind renewed I would begin to watch God drive this dude named 'Mocker' out of my soul. First he would be exposed for who he truly was; a fool, secondly his place of origin which was my arrogance and pride. And thirdly, his tactics which are such things as raising my voice, eye rolling, facial gestures, sarcasm and Bible quoting.

Though I have lived and roomed with him most of my life, I have never actually seen the 'Mocker'; but I bet he is one ugly dude! Maybe that's what southerners mean when they tell someone to stop being ugly! It means you are mocking and acting the fool! Mockers can be a 10 on the aesthetic scale but not even worth a second glance in life! Once the 'Mocker' inside is exposed all attractiveness goes out the window. Herein lies the truth, "Beauty is from the inside out!" Do you want to become more attractive in life? Then let God change you from the inside out. Not only will you become more attractive but you will have less strife as well. The toxic people who are attracted to the 'Mocker' won't be coming around as much. Mockers feed off one another. Healthy people are a hindrance to their way of living. The light of a healthy person exposes the 'Mocker' and that is his greatest fear.

I am also beginning to understand the importance of driving out the 'Mocker' when it comes to relationships. Not only can the 'Mocker' be ugly but he can be unhealthy too. And I mean unhealthy to the one he resides in as well as all those he wants to relate to. The 'Mocker' is a cancer on the road to relationships. That's why God had to drive this mocker from me before he could get me to 'Relationshipville!' Some of the 'Mockers' most cancerous traits are assigning motives and reading people's minds as if he actually knows what others are thinking. I know this first hand because I used to do it all the time. The 'Mocker' in me would always interpret situations through the lens of cynicism.

When I entered a conflict I would immediately assign motives to the others involved and then would begin to question them in order to get the answer I wanted or thought was the truth. In my mind I already knew the truth and why the other person did what they did or said what they said; after all I could read their mind! I'm tired just thinking about it. But that is the beauty of this journey of brokenness; it sets us free from ourselves! Imagine waking up in early January 2014 and trying to map this out! This journey of brokenness can't be mapped out; it can only be experienced! And though I am uncertain about the final destination of this journey, I am just going to walk it out. God is still holding my hand and promising to lead me to His best life possible.

So with the eyes of my heart wide open I say goodbye to 2014 and look forward with eager anticipation to what next year's leg of the journey will bring. We've added more bridges and lost a few folks along the way, but Jesus is still the same!

QUEST TO LOVE
Year Five

This year begins with a longing for something that has been missing from the first twenty years of walking with God and that is a deep sense of His love. I must admit I have tried everything under the sun to experience God's love. I have performed to earn it, abstained to feel it and sacrificed to justify it. Of course, none of these things truly helped me experience God's love and that is the crux of my problem. Love is not an emotion it's a choice! One has to choose to love and when that choice is made it can be felt! I have also come to know that it is not my love for God that is the game changer, but rather His love for me that changes all things.

So I ask the question in my quest to love, "What is love?" As I ask I realize that I already have the answer, "God is Love". But what exactly does that mean? What does that look like in my life? How do I come to believe that it is true? How do I experience it on a moment by moment basis? These are the questions that will ignite my quest to love and send me further along on my journey to the garden.

YEAR OF RESTORATION

As this year begins and my journey to the garden continues, a word has been revealed to me and is furthering the changes to my thought life: **Apokatastasis!** This is the Greek word for 'restoration' and means, "Restoration of true theocracy", or "Restoration to original intent". It just keeps appearing to me wherever I turn and it has powerful implications in my quest to love. You see, you and I were never meant to live in the wasteland; we were created to live in the garden. God created Adam and from Adam fashioned Eve. He then placed them in the garden to live and enjoy life and experience peace and communion with Himself (Genesis chapter 2). But Adam and Eve were deceived by Satan and disobeyed God's command to not eat from the 'Tree of knowledge of good and evil'.

Ever since our moment of rebellion lies have replaced the truth, shame has replaced righteousness and fear has driven out love. We humans were kicked out of the garden to live in the wastelands of the world where we toil and labor to no end to try and find paradise again. But I believe that is all about to change for me as I continue this journey to the garden with Hope as the anchor to my soul. But not only for myself, for all of God's people as we walk out this journey here on earth.

So let's talk about this word 'Apokatastasis' or the common English word restoration and why it is so important for our journey to the garden. It is always helpful to get somewhere when you have an idea of where you are going. It also allows you to relax and rest easier on the journey because you believe there is a purpose to the sojourn and its destination is good. So as the word restoration begins to seep into my mind and heart I sense that God is leading me back to the place I was originally intended to live, the garden! All of us were originally created to live in the garden communing with God and enjoying His abundant supply of provision for every area of life. Our spirits, souls and bodies weren't meant for this world in its fallen state. Our spirits were meant for life not death, our souls for peace not anxiety; and, our bodies for youth not decay. We were created to depend on God and not ourselves. But for me it has been a lifelong struggle of self-effort to provide and protect myself in hopes that I will survive till the end, my own death. But God doesn't want us surviving, He wants us thriving!

That was one of the major reasons I spent last year in Wrightsville Beach on the Island of Self-Love; **to move away from survival on my own to living in dependence on God!** My dependence on God needed to be restored. I had to say goodbye to the self-reliant "lone wolf McQuade" in me who took up residence on the Island of Self-Love. To do that I had to follow a seemingly illogical plan which involved selling all I owned and moving to an isolated beach hundreds of miles away. It turns out this move was a major step forward in the 'restoration of my life; my spirit, soul and body!

A second Greek word continues to seep into my soul: **Metanoeo!** It is the Greek word for 'repent', which means "to change one's mind, to think differently, to do an about face in ones thinking." This was a prominent theme last year as the Lord began to renew my mind in order to receive the restoration. A good part of the Lord's restoration in our life is done in our mind (the battlefield). I believe in order for God to restore us back to life in the garden, He must first get us to get our thoughts focused on Him rather than ourselves or this world. A Christ-conscience mind is necessary to a restored soul!

So how does the renewing of the mind and restoration fit together? I believe that as our mind begins to focus on God and starts to think as He does we are able to see the schemes the Enemy uses to steal what God has intended for us all along: our inheritance! I have had so much stolen from me by the Enemy because I simply listened to the lies he would whisper in my ear. It has caused me to trust the wrong kind of people, date the wrong kind of women, and hang with the wrong kind of crowd. But even more importantly it has caused me to keep the right kind of people out of my life and miss out on some truly wonderful opportunities.

That is all going to change! I am entering the fray and I am learning to fight for what is mine. I am on a quest to learn how to fight by learning to love! God is working to restore me to my intended original state of a sound mind and a pure heart! Galatians 5:6 says"… The only thing that counts is faith expressing itself through love." WOW! Stop and think about that for a minute. If the Creator of the universe tells us that what matters most is our love for God and others, why would we pursue anything else?!!! I have been looking for love my whole life and that's the problem: I've just been looking! Now the quest to love is on. This is an intentional pursuit to know what love is. And not just to know love, but to feel it, experience it and live it! Yes I am entering the fray and there is going to be a fight. But it's not a fight fought with an independent spirit and prideful will. No, it's a fight fought with a dependent spirit and surrendered will. The quest to love is a journey that requires humility and brokenness and it takes one further along on the journey to the garden.

So let the restorations of all things in my life begin! My quest to love is not going to be easy and will require some of the toughest battles I have ever fought. They are battles of forgiveness, reconciliation, meekness, humility and surrender. This battle requires a lover's grace, not a mocker's scorn, and is fought with the heart, not fists!

I WANT TO KNOW WHAT LOVE IS

My quest for love started 17 years ago one Sunday morning before church. I was in prayer and found myself having a discussion with God about Love and marriage. I don't remember the details of the conversation but do remember ending it with a prayer request, "I want to know what love is!" It was only a few minutes later that I turned on the radio in my car and what was playing - "I want to know what love is" by Foreigner! I could only sit with my head in my hands and laugh; Coincidence? I think not. Only God could time such a thing! At that moment I had a clear sense that God heard my prayer and answered it. Whatever circumstances God would bring about in order to teach me what love is were now set in motion.

Over the 17 years I would go through a myriad of trials to condition my heart to experience true love and begin to live like a loved person. The circumstances that God orchestrated in my life had a twofold purpose. The first involved tearing down the walls I had built to protect my heart from pain thereby exposing my fear of giving and receiving love. The second, focused on replacing the Enemy's lies with God's truth and restoring my heart to love unconditionally. To be honest I was so frustrated with this part of my journey. I went through so many trials and at the end of each one I would declare myself to finally 'be there' or to have 'arrived at love'. I must have done this a dozen times only to realize that I would be thrust into another trial or another relationship that would expose more of the same. I remember thinking to myself, "Will I ever get 'there?', or "when will I finally 'arrive' at loves' door? I believe I was looking for the formula of love and not love itself. If I could just make it through one final trial and get the last piece of the formula I could do it; I would have the ability to receive love and give it away. I would be a lover!

Let me promise you one thing, if you ever look to God for a formula for anything in life, especially love, you will embark on one of the most exhausting and frustrating journeys that a child of God will ever experience. The truth is, **Love is not a formula it is a choice!** There is nothing to figure out about love; with free will we simply get the privilege to choose it. The human heart was meant to love. That was its original intent before the fall. But in this broken and fallen world hearts get trampled on from a very early age and often take years or a lifetime to recover. But God is love, and love always perseveres. Therefore God is ruthless in His pursuit to recapture our hearts and restore them to love. So after 17 years of trials and failed relationships as a believer my heart had enough. I simply decided to walk up to the cross and lay my heart at Jesus' feet and say, "Lord, do with it what you will".

Now by this point in my journey to the garden God had already taught me the difference between an uncommitted heart and a committed heart (October 2013). But I had not traded in my uncommitted heart for the committed heart till I walked up to the cross and laid it at Jesus' feet in March 2014. As soon as I did that God immediately went into action teaching my new committed heart how to experience love by choosing it on a daily basis. Check this plan out!

LOVING MOM

Over the past year or so I had begun to see signs of dementia with my mom. Little things at first like repeating herself, and forgetfulness. Her condition worsened, however, into ever increasing episodes where she could not distinguish between what was real and what wasn't. I knew my siblings and I would be confronted with a whole new set of challenges in caring for her. I had no idea what my role might be besides extending financial support but God did and He was already at work in a special way I could never have foreseen.

Every March for the past several years I would buy my mom the 'MLB' package from her cable company so that she could watch all of her beloved NY Mets games. Little did I know she was such an avid baseball fan that she would even watch west coast games late at night no matter who the teams were; she simply loved to watch baseball! But this year was different. On the first day of the MLB season I called her to see if the package was working on her TV and realized that she was confused about the channels. She was unable to navigate the channels needed to watch her games. She even tried to change the channels with the phone instead of the remote which was quite loud in my ear! But then I heard that soft, quite voice of God whisper in my ear, "Here's what I want you to do; call your mom every day to help her find the channels, but also to tell her three words "I love you!" As soon as I heard those words I felt anxiety begin to course through my entire body.

I began immediately throwing up my defenses as to why I could not take on such a demanding request of my time and energy. How am I going to remember to call every day? My mom will think I have lost it if I call her every day! What will we talk about once she finds the channel? Those were just a few of my excuses. But then came the real resistance and it wasn't pretty!

I didn't want to call my mom every day. As a child I felt mistreated in many ways by my mom; verbally, mentally, spiritually and emotionally. It would come from all directions and in various forms. Screaming at me when I did something wrong even though I was never taught what was right. I was called every name in the book when my behavior wasn't perfect. I was rebuked for asking questions or smacked for not knowing the unknowable. It all left me walking on eggshells and afraid of what was around the corner. Then mix in my mom's psychic reading parties that I witnessed and you have a kid who feels confused, afraid, anxious and dirty all at the same time. God, you want me to call the person I blame for all my dysfunction and insecurities and tell her "I love you." And do it every day! Isn't that asking a bit much? I went on for hours trying to justify my position and defend my rights as a mistreated child. I even bargained with God that I was already healed of all the wounds through counseling and realized that my mom did what she thought was best for me and my siblings.

The pain she inflicted on me was coming from her own childhood pain, I get that and forgive her! Hurting people hurt people. So, why such a demanding request Lord? God's answer to that question was absolute silence! And in that silence I knew that the negotiations had ended and the only option left for me was obedience! I was going to have to trust that He knew what He was doing and that there was more to God's plan than my human mind could grasp. So then it began. A phone call a day, every day, to make sure my mom could find the channel for the NY Mets game and to make sure all was well!

Now, at first it seemed a little unnatural and I was nervous about her reaction to me calling every day. I always called my mom once a week on Sundays to check in, but would always hang up with a dark cloud feeling over my head, I had come to the conclusion that my mom was never going to change and I would just grin and bear it till the inevitable. It wasn't that I hated her or wished any harm to her; I just couldn't take any more reminders of my childhood. I needed to get as far away from it as possible and every call I made to her felt like I was being pulled back into the past and experiencing that pain that came with it. But as the daily phone calls started to pile up over the first several weeks and months, I began to notice a change in my mom that blew my mind! Pessimism began to change to optimism and the pity party turned to laughter! What in the world was happening?

I will tell you what was happening; 'perfect love was casting out fear!' I was witnessing it with my own eyes and hearing it with my own ears. Wow! And then it hit me, the words 'I Love You!' These three simple but powerful words spoken to someone every day can literally resurrect a heart from the grave! No wonder God asked me to call and say 'I love you' to my mom every day. He knows the power of our words. They can either build one up or tear one down. I watched this exchange of love for fear take place for an entire year and what has transpired is nothing short of a miracle!

In one year's time I have fallen in love with my mom! The daily phone call that I dreaded in the beginning has become the highlight of my day. I love to hear my mom laugh and talk about all the little things that now make her happy. We actually race each other to the words 'I love you' at the end of every call. We know that it's coming and can't wait for it. I see my mom in a whole new light and I know she feels more loved than ever before. God's plan of restoring my relationship with my mom back to its original intent was in full bloom! And I think that was a huge part of God's plan to teach me what love is! This is so important because if I am to love my future wife or any women God puts in my life I must have the original one working in proper order. If I couldn't love my mom unconditionally, how would I be able to love another woman unconditionally? And let me tell you, my relationships with not only women, but everybody, has begun to change and flourish ever since my relationship with my mom turned to one of unconditional love.

God makes this principal so very clear in the Bible. Ephesians 6:2-3 says, "Honor your father and mother"-which is the first commandment with a promise-"so that it may go well with you and that you may enjoy long life on the earth". How many times have I heard that before? Jesus said it! Moses said it! Matthew, Mark and Luke repeated it! If we will honor, obey and love our parents whom God chose specifically for us, we will enjoy the fruit of that love in every area of our lives for a very long time here on earth! Thank you Lord (Papa) for restoring the most important relationship I have on this earth to its original intent; unconditional love! And now that this relationship has been restored it's time to look at what is happening to my heart and its quest to love.

As a result of my restored relationship with my mom I have experienced tremendous healing in my heart; it has actually begun to feel again! All throughout this process I have noticed my relationship with God also change. Realizing the lengths He went to so I could move to Wrightsville Beach where He could pour out His love on me has done wonders for my heart. Ever since then I have not been able to take my eyes off of His love for me! And that is the point of it all; God's Love for me! In light of the past year's circumstances I have turned from focusing on my love for God, to God's love for me!

The days of trying to earn God's love through the works of the law are coming to an end in my life. God's love for me was exhibited at the cross where He gave His one and only begotten Son to die for me so that I may know what true love is; "no greater love than a man shall lay his life down for another!" Once you make that move away from the law (earning God's love through works) to grace (receiving His love by way of the cross) you will discover your heart begin to open up and receive the love it was meant to possess in the first place. And once the receiving of love begins to fill our hearts, the giving of love becomes the natural next step.

That is exactly what happened to me over this past year. As I realized that God loved me unconditionally I was able to begin loving others in the same way, especially my mom. And that lead me to discover another important aspect of love; that it is really a choice! Calling my mom to tell her that I love her was no longer something I felt I had to do to be obedient; it became a choice I decided to make every day! I chose to love by calling my mom. It was a choice I decided to make regardless of what was on the other end of the call.

That's the beauty of God's love for us; it frees us to love others unconditionally. We don't have to fear rejection or pain from others anymore because we already know and feel God's love for us! We are now free to choose love in any and all situations or relationships that come our way in life! That, my friends, is what true freedom is; "It is for freedom that Christ set us free." (Galatians 5:1) How about that! What I thought would be an exhausting and demanding task -- to call my mom every day and tell her 'I love you'-- has changed my life completely. Through my decision to choose love God has taught me what love is!

Before this past year I would read 1st Corinthians chapter 13 and come away confused and frustrated. But now God is teaching me every aspect of love. For example, one of my calls to my mom really ignited my quest to love by teaching me a couple of its attributes at the same time. We were searching for the channel that was airing the NY Mets game. For some reason my mom was having a particularly hard time focusing on the task of finding the right channel. Of course she was using the telephone to try and switch channels which really complicated the matter. Once I was able to settle her down and let her know she needed to put down the phone and pick up the remote I heard this soft quiet voice of a child say to me, "Oh honey, I'm sorry! I know I get confused at times but I don't mean too, please don't yell at me I'm just a little confused!" Wow!!! The thing here was that I had no intention of yelling at her. I had learned to be patient while she was in this state. But apparently she had felt the sting of correction so many times over the past several years from people, including myself that she felt the need to apologize.

She was a scared little girl just wanting to be loved and fighting loneliness and condemnation like the rest of us! It was at that moment I could hear the Holy Spirit whisper in my ear, "remember what you just heard and store it in your mind and heart!" So I did just that and her cry for help was now embedded deep in my heart and mind! After my mom and I finished our call and she was all set to watch her game, we said our 'I love you' and hung up. Immediately I began to repeatedly listen to what my mom had just said over and over again in my head. For some reason it was bringing me to my knees. I think it was the pain and despair I heard in her voice.

Then God did what only God can do! He took all of my negative childhood memories of my mom mistreating me verbally, emotionally, mentally and spiritually and wrapped them up into a single thought.

He then told me to hold it in my hand. "What did you learn from that conversation with your mom and her plea for mercy", He asked? My response was immediate. "I learned that "Love is not easily angered" and "It keeps no record of wrongs!" It was at that moment that an exchange occurred. He took the entire record of negative thoughts about my mom and replaced it with the memory of her words and cry for help. Now every time the Enemy brings up my past and the emotional wounds I suffered as a child, I hear the voice of my mom say "Oh honey, I'm sorry! I know I get confused at times but I don't mean too, please don't yell at me I just am a little confused!" And as I hear those words I fall deeper in love with my mom. That's restoration! That's fighting for love with love!

SYMPATHY TO EMPATHY

As my journey to the garden continues I realize there are still more bridges to cross. The first bridge on the horizon this past year spanned the gulf from 'Sympathy' to 'Empathy'. Of course I asked the question what's the point of crossing this bridge? What's the difference between sympathy and empathy, anyway?" Well, I was about to find out.

Webster's dictionary defines sympathy as feelings of pity and sorrow for someone else's misfortune. Empathy, on the other hand, is the ability to understand and share the feelings of another as well as the ability to see the world as others see it while being non-judgmental! Wow! I had no idea what a huge difference there was between the two. So I began to look into my own life and ponder whether I was sympathetic or empathetic.

Now it's not hard to see that I grew up in a home where I learned to be sympathetic. All the verbal mistreatment that I suffered caused me to build a wall of protection around me to shelter myself from pain, especially relational pain. I must have heard the words "Shame on you!" several hundred times growing up. I grew up in a shame based atmosphere that only allowed me to be sympathetic, in other words love from a distance and a safe enough distance not to get hurt. I read a quote somewhere, "Shaming people causes you to raise judgmental people!" And that is exactly what happened to me.

I developed into a perfectionist to avoid shame and expected everyone around me to be perfect as well. If they weren't I stepped in as judge, jury and executioner and let them know that what they were doing wrong. I could sympathize with their pain and would sometimes point out what I felt was their part in it and then simply walk away untethered! Let me say this out loud, "Sympathy exacerbates shame!!!" Pouring feelings of pity and sorrow on someone who is hurting without getting involved just makes the pain worse! Sympathy must be replaced with empathy. If sympathy exacerbates shame, then 'Empathy is the antidote to shame!

So what does empathy look like? Empathy is the ability to get involved with others and be vulnerable! Sympathy will look at a wounded soul down in a pit and say things like, "I'm so sorry! And "Oh, you poor thing!" But empathy doesn't say anything; it just crawls down in the pit and sits with the wounded soul. Empathy is where we truly feel others pain and are willing to sit in it with them. Empathy is showing up and getting involved in other people's lives: the good, the bad and the ugly! I am now aware that empathy requires vulnerability, and vulnerability is our most accurate measure of courage! So again I see love at work here; it's driving out my fear of vulnerability! You can't give empathy without vulnerability. I must be willing to be vulnerable to be empathetic.

So how does someone who fears vulnerability learn to be vulnerable? First I believe that we have to understand why we fear vulnerability and what defense mechanisms we have developed to cope. It's pretty obvious that mine is perfectionism! And where there is perfectionism there is always shame. Perfectionism is a thought process that says, "If I look perfect, do perfect, live perfect, work perfect and do it all perfectly, I can avoid or minimize shame, blame, judgement and criticism." Perfectionism keeps us imprisoned to our self and prevents us from experiencing life. Perfectionism is all about external validity. It is the opposite of healthy living. The French writer Voltaire said, "Perfectionism is the enemy of good."

So I ask myself the question; what causes me to be a perfectionist? It is my desire for certainty! Wow!!! Why certainty Papa? Because I have lived my entire life in uncertainty! Remember, earlier in the journey I talked about how I would get infuriated as a kid when my mom uttered the words "because I said so!" I never was willing to do anything unless I knew why I had to do it. I was really frozen by uncertainty; I didn't know how to trust and obey. But to really understand empathy I will need to overcome my perfectionist tendencies and let go of my uncertainties in life. Wouldn't you know it that was the next bridge God laid before me!

UNCERTAINTY TO CERTAINTY

If I am going to become an empathetic person it is going to require vulnerability. But in order to be vulnerable I am going to have to let go of uncertainty. But what does it take to let go of uncertainty? Once again I can hear the Holy Spirit speaking it to me loud and clear; **Clarity!** I kept hearing that word over and over again for the past eighteen months. It all started with a conversation I had with my pastor regarding pre-marital sex. I wanted to know why some Christians chose to abstain while others chose to engage in such activity. His response was a revelation. "My friend, purity gives you clarity! That's why Jesus said, "Blessed are the pure in heart, for they will see God." (Mathew 5:8)" Clarity trumps uncertainty because clarity lets you **SEE** where you're going, even when you don't **KNOW** where you are going! And that my friend is what allows Gods children to walk by faith! (Hebrews 11:1)

Clarity is the vision needed to cross the bridge from 'Uncertainty' to 'Certainty'. When I am in a state of uncertainty such things as doubt, apprehension, reservation, suspicion and second thoughts rule my mind. They create a fog and paralyze me. I can't move forward in life because I have zero visibility. But to move into a state of certainty with confidence, sureness, positivity and conviction would give me the clarity to move forward.

So how do I know when uncertainty is paralyzing me and how do I overcome it? So often when faced with a major decision I would poll others for their opinions. The more the better, but in reality the more people I polled, the more I got confused and ultimately paralyzed. That's when God intervened! The key to overcoming paralysis and finding clarity is elimination! AHA!!! No wonder God has been talking to me about getting rid of distractions. All year long I have had a prevailing theme in my mind that keeps telling me, "no more drama!" "Get rid of the distractions!" And now it is starting to make sense. Get rid of the distractions and clarity will take its place. It goes without saying that now I am learning to be a lot more careful about whose opinion, and how many, I seek.

Okay, so now I have chosen certainty over uncertainty by eliminating distractions. What does that get me? Again we defer to the Holy Spirit and I believe His answer is; Clarity! Having clarity allows you to be vulnerable! There you go! In order to be an empathetic person you must have clarity which allows you to be vulnerable enough to show up in other people's lives. At that point you are on life's right path and that path is paved with **certainty!**

I am willing to be certain now and I know I am on the right path; good things are about to happen! I have clarity! I have hope! I have let go of the lie that I will finally arrive there at love's door one day. The truth is I can choose love now! I get the privilege to show up for life everyday day and be vulnerable. It is not easy to be on this path; it is definitely the road less traveled and requires perseverance. I believe this is a season in which I am learning perseverance as I cross the numerous bridges in front of me. The only way I know how to develop perseverance is to persevere! And to do so requires spending a lot of time alone with God in silence; quiet time! What also excites me is to see the fruit of crossing previous bridges begin to blossom in my life. I see the lessons of the bridge from an 'uncommitted heart' to a 'committed heart' surface. I am looking for solutions to keep going, where in the past I would be planning my escape from this difficult path! With the perseverance of my new committed heart I look to further my career; enjoy my existing relationships; cherish my family and continue trusting God even when I don't understand the way forward!

It was a long twenty-six months. From March 1st 2013 through May 1st 2015 I lived in a suitcase. I shared earlier that I was led by God to sell my house a few years ago as part of plan for Him to reconstruct my life in order to receive His best. And as you know I ended up dividing the next 26 months between staying with friends in Atlanta and living at the beach in North Carolina. During that period I never felt settled enough to unpack my suitcase. Every time I arrived at one of my living arrangements I already had my next trip planned. The stay never lasted more than three weeks.

So I lived out of the suitcase. For someone who had lived in his own home for 12 years, living as a nomad came with some adjustments. But it also came with a freedom that is hard to explain. It gave me a whole new perspective on stuff! I no longer had the desire to keep all the stuff I had accumulated over a lifetime. I ended up giving away about seventy-five percent of all I owned and can't wait to get rid of the rest! It was an extremely long stretch of transition, but it has been worth it. It's was now time for me to unpack my suitcase!

So here it is, May 1st 2015 and I am unpacking my suitcase for the first time in 26 months. I finally have my very own place to call home for now. And then I hear it, the Holy Spirit whispering, "As you unpack your suitcase and settle in over the next few months, we will also be unpacking all you have been through spiritually!" Wow!!! I had this sense that everything about me was changing. The way that I perceived life, the way I thought about God and others, the type of women I was interested in, the way I looked at my friendships and how I conducted business. Every aspect of life and my perception of it seemed to be different but I could not for the life of me figure out why.

Then, out of nowhere it happened: the lights went out! And I mean total darkness as well as complete silence! I was in isolation! Yikes!!! I had ended my last dating relationship without a trace of a new one in sight. My business came to a complete stop. My friends all but disappeared. I had nowhere to go and no one to see. I went into one of the loneliest times of isolation that I had ever experienced. That's how I spent the summer of 2015, in the darkness of deep isolation. God had my attention!

In mid-September 2015 I was having a conversation with a friend and sharing how I felt about my life and the experience of being in isolation this past summer. I told him I had found myself repeating the phrase, "everything is changing." He responded with, "Why don't you try saying 'everything HAS changed?' You're not the same person you used to be"! For some reason that just rocked me! It resonated deep in my heart and I realized it was true. I wasn't the same person and that's why I was seeing and perceiving everything differently now. I had a new set of eyes and ears and felt a greater sense of freedom than ever before.

Everything had changed! I was a completely new person but I was unsure what to do with that. I asked God, "What happened?" He said, "You have emerged! You have survived and broken out of chrysalis! You are now a butterfly and no longer a caterpillar! You have become the person I had originally intended you to be." But I still had to ask the question, "Why such a dark time of isolation?" So I studied a bit more on the chrysalis and learned that after a butterfly emerges from chrysalis it needs time (24 hours) to remain in darkness and allow for its wings to harden so that they may be useful for flying! That is why after exiting the chrysalis stage myself, I went into a dark time of loneliness and isolation for the entire summer. My wings were hardening, (my character was being solidified). I had become the butterfly and was getting ready to fly and live free.

In 2012 I wrote about how I felt I was entering into a chrysalis stage in my life. The long and arduous self-occupied life I was living was coming to an end and I needed to change. But I was clueless as to the plan that God was using for my development, or better said, my brokenness. But that is the beauty of God's plan of brokenness. It allows God to lead us through places and to places that we would never go on our own. Just think about it for a moment; who wants to get rid of their 'self'? We are all we have ever known! Being ourselves and living for ourselves is how we are taught to live and survive in this world, a world where we "look out for number one!" To let go of that and live by faith seems unnatural and somewhat scary. It is about giving up control and when we do that we get scared!

We have talked about the 'illusion of control' earlier and know it's a lie. We are never in total control, God is. So when we give up the false belief of control we are actually going back to the original way we were meant to live with God leading the way and us under His protection. In the darkness of my chrysalis, God was killing me off! He was killing my self-life in order to bring about the life of Christ in me! Again we see the beauty of brokenness at work. Brokenness allows God to lead us to the chrysalis stage where true transformation can take place. Now the chapter "We need to talk" that I wrote back in 2012 makes pure sense. My flesh, my self-life had lost all power, I was running on fumes and barely had any life in me left. Now I know why I cried out to God to do whatever it took to rescue me from my own life. It wasn't working anymore! It also makes sense now why God asked me to let go and give everything up to him. He told me it was going to look and feel as if everything was falling apart but to not be anxious or afraid.

The truth was God was transforming me to live the best life possible; His way! It takes transformation to get us ready to receive all God has for us and it takes the chrysalis stage to be transformed! I will be honest, it takes real courage to enter chrysalis! And I believe it is brokenness that gives us that courage. Strong willed believers if put into a state of chrysalis will try to fight their way out prematurely. As soon as the darkness and the trials that come during that stage get to be too much, they will try to regain control by busting out of the chrysalis. Resting and trusting God during chrysalis takes patience, commitment, courage and perseverance. Perseverance is especially needed. In chrysalis, life is all about resting and being still while everyone and everything apparently passes you by. But perseverance is what it takes so that God can complete the transformation process and we can emerge as butterflies

DE-STUMPING THE SOUL

After the amazing revelation I just experienced from my emergence from chrysalis, the gardening of my soul would now kick into high power. There was some stumping to do in my heart. For the past five years God had been pulling weeds and clearing the thistles, thorns and briers that were growing in the garden of my heart. My soul was in the early stages of being transformed from a wasteland to a garden. It was now time to uproot and crush all the remaining roots and stumps in my soul. It was now time to clear my heart for a good crop producing thirty, sixty or a hundredfold. It's time for God to break out the ripper-tooth!

One might ask the question, "Why is this stage of clearing the land so important?" Because if a stump and its roots belong to a tree that is a lie, like condemnation, you do not want that root left in the ground! It will eventually grow back and be restored into your soul. There are many lies that have grown in the garden of my heart and soul, but condemnation is the largest. It must be de-stumped, up-rooted and crushed!

This all became apparent after emerging from my chrysalis when I was still trying to live like a caterpillar; it felt extremely unnatural and awkward. I had to come to the realization that I was a butterfly. The deep rooted stumps of lies, especially condemnation, did not feel natural anymore and had to be removed! It was time for me to repent and change the way I see, feel and think about myself.

So I began to ask myself the following questions; "What are my core beliefs about myself? Not what I know to be true, but what do I really believe to be true about me?" The old me would say that I know that

God loves me, but sometimes disapproves of my behavior! Therefore I am now under condemnation because my relationship with God is based on behavior not standing or identity and my behavior wasn't always pretty! Just look at the definition of condemnation, "a statement or expression of very strong and definite criticism or disapproval." That's not how God sees me! That's a lie! God loves me unconditionally; that's the truth! And now that I am free as a butterfly to believe the truth, that is exactly how I see myself; totally, completely and unconditionally accepted and loved by God! Goodbye stump of condemnation! And when that huge stump gets uprooted there will be plenty of space and fresh soil to plant new seeds, which all will become fruit bearing plants. These are seeds that are the opposite of condemnation. Seeds like commend, absolve, approve, praise, exonerate, pardon, release and set free! These are all the counter seeds to condemnation and will bring about the opposite effect. When these seeds bloom they will send out pollen that smells like love! Yes, 'Love is in the air'!

So it is here at the end of my chrysalis and in the midst of my quest to love that I hear God say to me, "Enough is enough my child, you are enough and there is now no condemnation for you because of Jesus, as we are reminded of in Romans 8:1! You are so loved!!!" Knowing that there is no longer any condemnation is the gateway to life in the spirit! It opens the door to let love in and permeate every square inch of our heart. We finally get to show up for life. We are set free to live life as a loved person and fly like a butterfly. Like Mark Twain said, "Dance like no one's watching, Sing like no one's listening, Love like you've never been hurt, Live like's it heaven on earth." And that's just what I'm going to do!

I don't want to be naïve. I know the Christian life, even when lived with a healthy heart and the freedom of a butterfly has its tests and trials. Removing condemnation and replacing it with vulnerability and love will entail a fight. We have already learned the lesson last year that it is easier to keep the Enemy out of the garden than it is to remove him from territory he has claimed for years! The Enemy knows that vulnerability is a difficult emotion for us and it is easy for him to get us to fear it. But vulnerability is also the birthplace of every positive emotion we want in our lives. Ridding our hearts of condemnation will also empower us to further cross the bridge from a 'Mocker' to a 'Lover'. In doing so peace will begin to spread throughout the garden of our hearts like wildfire!

UNTANGLING ONESELF FROM MOCKERS

Earlier this year I found myself falling to my knees and praying to God, "No more drama!" I had enough drama in my life to last seven lifetimes. And I know it came from being one of the most prolific mockers this world has ever seen. I had mastered my mockery skills very well having grown up in a tough environment. That coupled with the defense mechanisms I developed as a result of the emotional mistreatment I endured as a child made me into a ninja in the art of mockery. I was once told that I could freeze a person out, you know make them disappear even though they were right in front of me, better than anyone in the world. If I didn't want you to exist and be part of my world I could put you on ice and not think twice about you. Just receiving that so called compliment fueled my mockery even more. I wasn't able to see that as a fault or weakness, to me it was pure strength and the ability to stand my ground!

After hearing that I was a master at the freeze out I would have to literally walk through doorways sideways because my chest and arms would be so puffed up I couldn't walk straight through. The freeze out is just one of the ways a mocker invites drama into their life. Last year I talked about the many mocker techniques there are as I was being introduced to the bridge crossing over from a 'Mocker' to a 'Lover'. What I had discovered as I began to cross that bridge is that by using these mocker techniques, you are inviting drama into your life. Freezing people out, sarcasm, eye rolling, dogmatism, black and white thinking, raising one's voice, and back door insults and of course bible quoting to justify oneself are not peacemaker's, rather they are invitations to drama!

So after my prayer for 'no more drama', I believe God's response was to untangle myself from the mocker within, as well as the mockers in my life. We already know from proverbs that to drive out the mocker is to get rid of strife, quarrels and insults, which are all results of fear. And if perfect love drives out fear, I believe we have a plan. Therefore if you want to drive out the mocker the lover must develop within you.

Now in order to continue to drive out the mocker I was going to have to give up one of my favorite types of candy; M&M's! Which stands for 'mocker moves!' Picture it this way. It's like I am walking around as a lover, but still carrying a bag of M&M's in my pocket just in case I need to defend myself in any situation or crisis that might occur. If I continue to walk around and claim to be a lover, but yet still carry this bag of 'Mocker Moves', what I am really saying is that I want to appear to be a lover but the real me, the mocker, can come out at any time! A true lover doesn't walk around with the M&M's in his pocket; he has to dump the bag. A lover must untangle himself from those mockers moves or they will eventually resurface and cause, you got it, drama!

What I have also discovered during this year is that lovers and mockers do not mix well together. They live in different realities. Mockers exist in drama, while lovers live in peace! Mockers need other mockers to fuel their fury and pride. They need to hang together and have a good old gripe session, dine on some gossip and cut someone down to pieces who's not around. Lovers attract other lovers and will get together for mutual edification. Lovers are interested in the person they are with at the moment. What I am truly discovering about my quest to love and desire to be a lover is that you can't just claim to be a lover and try to act like one; you must actually transform from a mocker to a lover!

So the dis-entanglement begins! And in order to untangle myself from the mocker within and the mockers without, I must also understand that the mocker himself has many facets. There is the business mocker, the friendship mocker, the dating mocker and the family mocker. The mocker can show up in all four of these areas of life. For instance, business mockers will always do what is in their own economic best interests regardless of the people it hurts. Individual businessman will sometimes do this under the guise of 'I have to protect my family' or 'I have to protect what's mine!' What they are really saying is being right is more important than doing right! Be careful what agreements you enter into with the business mocker. A bad deal can be very hard to untangle! The friendship mocker will always do what is right for their side of the friendship. They will demand one-hundred percent blind loyalty and will often expect others to meet on their time and at their chosen locations. They will also expect others to entangle themselves in their own personal lives and agendas. It's their way of getting a sense of belonging, albeit an unhealthy one.

Friendship mockers don't come with contracts but can be extremely difficult to untangle once you are connected. In many instances disentanglement from the friendship mocker can get quite nasty because they will see such efforts as betrayal. This is typically displayed by them with the fight or flight syndrome. The dating mocker is someone who really doesn't go out on dates, they go out on interviews. They typically are looking for faults and not loving attributes. It's more about having their date prove to them why they should see them again, rather than 'are we a good fit?' The dating mockers already know they have their side of the relationship taken care of; all is good on their end! So be careful not only about dating a mocker, but be extra careful not to marry one.

And then there is the family mocker and it seems every family has one. You know, the one the rest of the family says, "so and so is all about themselves! Never calls anyone but expects to be called and only calls when they need something! It's always friends before family with this one! Shows up for the good times and disappears for the tough times!" Untangling one's self from the family mocker is extremely difficult because chances are you have spent a lot of time with them, know them well and are obligated to the relationship through blood!

I know deep down in my heart that this process is going to take a while and I am totally prepared to see it through. I learned the art of patience (another attribute of love) from being a fisherman for the past 25 years. I can't tell you how many times I have had to sit on a boat and untangle my line in order to make another cast. I have learned that if you take your time and gently remove one tangle at a time you will eventually get the whole knot out, but it may take a while. It is especially hard to be patient when your fishing partner has found the perfect fishing hole and is landing one fish after another!

DRAMA IS TOXIC LOVE

We weren't meant for it; not our spirit's, not our hearts, our souls nor our bodies. Toxic love is just what it says it is; Toxic! It is a deadly and poisonous emotion that will make you sick spiritually, mentally, emotionally and physically! I want to share with you some powerful quotes from Dr. Caroline Leaf, a Christian Neurologist who has spent 30 years studying the mind with the help of the scriptures. First quote, "We are not designed for toxic love. Distorted toxic love is learned fear and completely blocks our gifts. Healthy love on the other hand rewires the brain, increasing our health, intelligence and happiness. When our love circuit fires, it is more difficult for the learned fear to fire at the same time. When we move into Godly love, things don't bother us as much and we simply love being in love."

That is a powerful statement of why we want to get rid of toxic love. Quote number two, "As I have now said many times, choice is greater than any learned pattern of negative or selfish love. And as we choose to change to healthy love, dopamine and oxytocin increase and start melting down the old connections to prepare the way for the new ones. Science is showing us that there is a massive unlearning of negative toxic thoughts when we operate in love. The brain releases a chemical called oxytocin, which literally melts away the negative toxic thought clusters so that rewiring of new non-toxic circuits can happen. This chemical also flows when we trust and bond and reach out to others: So love wipes out fear!"

Wow! Do you see why the renewing of the mind and driving out the mocker and fear are so important to becoming a lover! And finally quote number three," When we do good and reach out in love, God blesses us by helping our brains detox and increasing our motivation and wisdom thereby helping us negotiate life more successfully!" Look at that! Becoming a lover and learning to live in that love will help us to be successful in every facet of life; business, friendship, dating, marriage and family! Love not only untangles us from mockery and fear, it tangles us up with God so that when others see us they will see God as well! This is fascinating!

GRIEVING THE MOCKER

It's time to say goodbye to the mocker in me. I have been through this grieving process before and will probably go through it several more times. But it is necessary and must take place if we grow and mature in life. I went through this process when I accepted Jesus as my Lord and Savior twenty-one years ago. I had to grieve the old self so that I could become the new creation God created me to be. In that process I lost many friends and relationships that were tied to my old way of life. Some wanted nothing to do with me anymore, they chose flight! Others stuck around and tried to keep me from breaking free. They thought I had lost my mind and tried to talk me out of this new way of life. They used guilt and shame to try and hold me down, "you'll never change", "it's just a phase", "you hypocrite! We know the real you!" They all chose to fight! But some stuck around and chose love! They are all still good friends today, some believers and some not. But we are still friends and they are all examples to me of true friendship and what love can do when change occurs.

I also had to go through this grieving process soon after I was broken when I first realized that I was leaving the wasteland and headed to the garden. The wasteland was the only home I had ever known. No matter how miserable it was, it was still my home! Salvation had me grieve in my spirit, brokenness first had me grieve my location (from wasteland to garden) and now it is having me grieve my soul (from mocker to lover)! And as I grieve God has put another bridge in my path!

BEHAVIOR MODIFICATION TO CHARACTER TRANSFORMATION

In order for me to truly say goodbye to the mocker within I will no longer be able to participate in behavior modification. I will now have to allow character transformation to form me from the inside out. This has become evident to me as I emerged from the chrysalis this year. I knew I had changed on the inside because nothing in my life felt or looked the same. But it wasn't about location or anything my eyes could see; it was about perspectives; as a newly formed butterfly and a lover my perspective was changing. It was a perspective that came from hope, a confident expectation of good! This hope allowed me to see the good in others and not their faults. It's the perspective of a lover. But it didn't come from anything that I did. It came from who I became. That's what the bridge from 'behavior modification' to 'character transformation' does; it gives you a brand new perspective on life!

The way God explained this process of transformation was really cool and made clear to me what really had taken place during chrysalis. When I became a believer in Jesus Christ in 1994, my identity and standing with God had completely changed; I just didn't realize it! I remember saying to myself, "Okay, now I am a Christian, but I am still me. All I have to do is behave like a Christian and I will fit right in with the rest of the believers." I thought all I had to do was change the way I acted. I needed to stop doing certain things altogether and change the way I did some other things. I also needed to start doing certain things because 'that's what Christians do!' I had to do them whether I wanted to or not, or whether I liked it or not; they just had to be done and the more the better! It was a brutal and exhausting way to live and after fifteen years I finally ran out of gas and broke down. Thank you once again Papa for that gift of brokenness!

What I was doing for those fifteen years was modifying my behavior. It was like trying to glue a pair of wings on a caterpillar! You can try to make it look like a butterfly but it's still going to be a caterpillar. Gluing on a pair of wings won't make the caterpillar fly nor will it turn it into a butterfly. The only way for the caterpillar to become a butterfly is through the process of transformation which takes place during chrysalis! What changes one's life is transformation!

Now a caterpillar will completely change its outward appearance as it transforms into a butterfly. As humans, our transformation takes place completely on the inside. It is the landscape of our heart that is transformed which cannot be seen by the naked eye and therefore must be something experienced by others to realize we have changed. Your average everyday casual observer may not notice right away or even spend the necessary time to observe the change in you, but broken people will! Broken people can recognize other broken people almost immediately. They recognize the attributes of brokenness like a contrite and surrendered heart, a sense of humility and a sincere interest in others wellbeing. There is an understanding that this broken person is a safe person with healthy boundaries.

The first thing people will encounter when they meet a broken soul that has gone through the transformation and become a lover is Jesus. Encountering Jesus is God's goal when he breaks the will of one of His children and takes them through the restoration of their soul and the transformation to a lover. He wants others to encounter His Son first before they are to be touched by our soul; that is the purpose of the separation of the soul and spirit! Remember, God wants His message of grace to freely flow out of His chosen ones on earth. That's why God doesn't immediately take us to heaven once we are saved. We are called to be ambassadors of

Christ to the rest of this fallen world. We are called to be lovers and safe people. Every bit of testing and breaking that I went through in the past five years was worth it to become the person I am today, and the journey is still not over! The separation of my soul from my spirit will become more evident as I continue to have my soul restored into its original state.

BEING FOUND BY LOVE

As this year comes to a close I can't help but feel that love has finally found me. That scared little boy who crawled into his hiding place at the age of three has been found. It was a long time coming but the result of a loving God who was and still is on a rescue mission to restore my heart to its original design! He sent the greatest lover of all to rescue you and me, His one and only Son Jesus Christ! The beauty of this restoration of my heart is that it went all the way down to the root of the problem; condemnation! Love de-stumped that root and has begun to drive out all of the lies and fears condemnation caused to grow in my heart. Love has transformed me from a mocker to a lover who now see's others as purposely created beings made in the image of God rather than obstacles to my life!

Love is now the all-consuming thought in my mind. I awake every day to the same prayer, "How can I love like God loves today?" I can't wait to step out into the world and into love. With my new eyes I look for opportunities to love all day long. My deepest longing to know what love is has become a reality in my life. My dream has come true! Proverbs 13:12 says it well, "Hope deferred makes the heart sick, but a longing fulfilled is a tree of life." How wonderful is that?!!! Again scripture is coming to life in me. Just look at all the truths of that verse that are happening in my life. I discovered hope in 2013 which has allowed my heart to heal so as to no longer be sick.

My longing to know love has been fulfilled which has changed the landscape of my heart back to a garden. And there is life in the garden, not death! This verse even mentions the tree of life, the tree which is at the center of the Garden of Eden. I think our journey to the garden is really getting close and God is beginning to give us a glimpse of what is to come. What a beautiful year of discovering love! It is love that cures all and God is love!

> "Love makes your soul crawl out from its hiding Place!"
> -Zora Neale Hurston-

HEARING HEART

As my heart of love prepares to enter the year 2016 I feel a deep need for wisdom. Ever since I emerged from chrysalis as a butterfly all things have become new. I have new eyes that give me a new perspective to see as God sees. And now that I can see with clarity, I want to hear better as well. I have new ears and want them to be adjusted to hear God and hear Him only. I want to cut off the noise and lies of the Enemy. I won't have it anymore! I need wisdom and it comes from a hearing heart! Having the soil of my heart healed and turning it from bad to good readies it for the next step: the planting of the seeds of wisdom! Luke 8:15," But the seed on good soil stands for those with a noble and good heart, who **hear** the word, retain it, and by persevering produce a crop." It's time to begin producing a crop God's way! Therefore I ask you Lord: Please give me a hearing heart!

SEARCH FOR WISDOM
Year Six

This year I have an overwhelming sense that my emotions are going to be front and center in God's restoration of my soul. "The search for wisdom" and the "development of emotional IQ" are the themes resonating in my soul. I know that wisdom is the character of God (truth) applied to life. It also comes from spending time with God and making friends with the Holy Spirit! I have a deep desire to begin to apply wisdom to my life and something deep down in my soul tells me that my emotions must be dealt with in order for that to happen. I have more of a desire to know the thoughts of God; Einstein once said, "I want to know God's thoughts – the rest are mere details." I have also come to the conclusion that our thoughts must precede our emotions in order to properly manage our way through life. I am learning to hear God's voice above all things and to stop listening to the Enemy! We produce an evil crop by first listening to the Enemy's lies, second, believing them to be true, and then manifesting it in our lives! Satan laughs at us when we believe and act out a lie! And I am sick and tired of being laughed at!

So now I hear the Lord telling me it's time to change my perspective when it comes to the lies of the Enemy. When we recognize that we are led astray by sin or have listened to the lies of the Enemy, it's okay because we are now aware of something in our life that we need to get rid of! There's no shame in acknowledging sin in our lives, it is an opportunity to repent and mature!

So stop listening to the Enemy's lies and begin to apply wisdom to your life and your emotions will follow. Emotions are indicators of things that are wrong and right. Again, we are not to lead with our emotions; we are to lead with wisdom in our thinking. Using a train analogy - wisdom is the engine and our emotions are the caboose!

Can't wait to see where the journey leads. I'll be searching for wisdom and watching God deal with my emotions. Wisdom can be found in the most unlikely places and emotions can come out of nowhere when they are not under the authority of God. This year ought to be quite interesting.

HE PREPARED A NEW PLACE

The year 2016 starts off with a bang and here we go again! My suitcase unpacked for only eight months and it's time to pack again. Though it was a result of the loss of a dear friend, I am moving to Gainesville, GA. My dream of moving to the country is finally becoming a reality. I have acquired another custom clothing business and will transition my life and career to the North Georgia Mountains! It is truly amazing to watch the hand of God work in my life. He had me move to the beach two and a half years ago to shut all the doors to my past and begin to walk me toward my future. Now He has me moving to a small town in North Georgia and is opening doors to my future that has me running at full sprint just to get to the open doors on time! The past 7 plus years of my life have been brutal! I often wondered if I was going to make it through. I suffered physically, emotionally, mentally, financially, vocationally and spiritually.

The brokenness I suffered in January of 2010 was so painful I thought I was going to die and thanks to God I did. I died to myself and my flesh and was crucified with Christ (Galatians 2:20). I was finally able to see what had truly taken place on the cross. God immediately began to teach me to hear his voice above all things in life. It is the very first lesson we learn as broken people because it is the most important characteristic of a mature child of God. My ears are getting more accustomed to the voice of God as I intentionally 'incline my ears toward Him' (Proverbs 4:20) and pay careful attention to His instruction.

I am at the point in this journey where I have no desire to make any moves without first hearing from God; I need Him to lead me! Walking through the past 7 years of darkness with one trial after another will train you to hear God's voice. That is exactly what has happened with me. The prophet Isaiah said it best, "Although the Lord gives you the bread of adversity and the water of affliction, your teachers will be hidden no more; with your own eyes you will see them. Whether you turn to the right or the left, your ears will hear a voice behind you saying, "This is the way; walk in it." (Isaiah 30:20)

So now I am entering a season of this journey where God is restoring back to me territory that the Enemy had stolen from me. His promise of restoring all things, "apokatastasis" last year's theme is in full affect. I have an opportunity to regain all the business I lost three years ago and more, plus move to the type of place I would want to live and raise a family. But let me assure you there is going to be a fight. The Enemy never gives up ground he has taken from us very easily. It seems like **it is a hundred times harder to get the Enemy out of your land than it is to keep him out!** So in order to possess the territory that truly belongs to me, I am going to need wisdom and courage to retake it from the Enemy!

Hence, 'the search for wisdom' has begun. And with it comes the need for the development of healthy emotions. As I said before I felt as if I was mistreated and neglected emotionally as a child and now the time has come for the healing and balancing of my emotions to take place. This will require God to untie all the knots in my heart that cause my emotions to interfere with God's plan for my life. So Papa, "grant me the wisdom to follow You in this season of my journey. Give me a hearing and understanding heart that I may know You and Your will for my life!"

"My son, do not let wisdom and understanding out of your sight,
preserve sound judgement and discretion; they will be life for you
an ornament to grace your neck. Then you will go on your way
in safety, and your foot will not **stumble**." (**Proverbs 3:21**)

NO MORE STUMBLING

It is starting to become clear to me why I have stated over and over again that I have felt as if I have been alone since the age of three. I'm getting the picture in my mind that as far back as I can remember (my earliest childhood memory) I put myself into isolation in order to survive the chaos of my childhood. I found a deep dark cave in the corner of my heart and went into hiding the minute my mind was able to figure that out, even as early as the age of three. All of my life isolation and loneliness were a safe place for me. But in the past two years the isolation became so painful that something had to be done. I went into isolation as a very young child to protect myself from pain. But what ended up happening was the isolation became the root cause of my pain. I had reached the point where isolation was no longer safe; it was actually now more painful than the risk of love and relationships. I had become sick and tired of surviving in my cave; my heart began to desire life. Jesus didn't die on the cross so I could survive till the end, He gave His life so that I could live and have life in an abundant way! That was the purpose of last year's 'quest for love'. God's perfect love (1st John 4:19) would cast out all my fear and allow me to crawl out from my hiding place unafraid. I am sick and tired of surviving and it is time for me to live.

So I ask the question, "What caused me to crawl into a dark lonely cave of isolation at the age of three?" I sense the Lord's answer to me was "emotional neglect!" That was the root cause of my isolation. Hiding was my defense mechanism against the pain of rejection. The fact that my father wasn't around much when I was a child because of he spent almost every night away gambling at the racetracks left me feeling neglected and unwanted. I know he didn't mean to leave me with those feelings, in his mind he was trying to earn more money to make our lives better; it just didn't work out so well! I had a hard time handling what I felt was rejection and didn't know what to do with my emotions. If I tried to express those feelings to my mom who was home alone, I was immediately shut down; it was probably the only way she knew how to handle her pain and loneliness. By doing so, her pain and loneliness would be transferred to me and leave me in tears. Then all I would hear were the words, "stop your crying or I will give you something to cry about!" It was a vicious cycle of pain and we all suffered from it in our own way.

My response was to crawl down into my cave and be alone with my thoughts and feelings; it was the only safe place I could find! I believe that's where the Enemy found his way into my heart; I was completely alone and totally defenseless. It was then that he began to take possession of my heart and establish it with his lies. Sitting there alone hearing the Enemy's lies gave me a negative view of myself and that allowed condemnation, guilt and shame to settle in my heart! "Something must be wrong with me!" "Nobody loves me!" "I am better off alone!" I just shut down emotionally and became 'emotionally unavailable'. Condemnation left me hopeless and shame told me that something was wrong with me; therefore I better not let anyone find out who I really was. This of course led to isolation! And to top it off, guilt gave me an expectation of punishment whether I did something wrong or not. And I believe the constant expectation of punishment led me to develop into a perfectionist. A perfectionist has to have everything in perfect order, including themselves and the people around them, as a protection against disappointment and punishment. There can be no mistakes, omissions or any sense of anything less than perfect; or else!

That is what a stressed out home life can do to a young child; it can cause him to 'stumble' through life as a perfectionist; hence the word 'stumble'. Stumble means our conscience is trained to believe lies (untruths)! When I sat all alone in my cave the Enemy trained me to believe his lies. In the Greek language, the word 'stumble' is SKANDALON. It is where we get the English word SCANDAL, definition; an action or event regarded as morally wrong and causing outrage. There you have it! Beginning at an early age I was caught up in a scandal! The Enemy worked through my parents and in my heart to cause me to stumble, to believe lies about God, them and myself! Wow!!! I believe I have finally discovered the root cause of all my pain and fears!

So after receiving the revelation for the root cause of my pain, what now? Where do we go from here Papa? How do we restore all the lies back to truth? How do we gain back all those years of living in isolation and fear? I believe the answer to these questions is found in Matthew chapter 18 in the first nine verses! It is where the disciples are debating who will be 'the greatest in the kingdom of heaven.' Jesus gives His answer;

He called a little child to him, and placed the child among them. And he said: "Truly I tell you, unless you change and become like little children, you will never enter the kingdom of heaven. Therefore, whoever takes the lowly position of this child is the greatest in the kingdom of heaven. And whoever welcomes one such child in my name welcomes me." (Mathew 18: 3-4)

"If anyone causes one of these little ones-those who believe in me-to stumble, it would be better for them to have a large millstone hung around their neck and to be drowned in the depths of the sea. Woe to the world because of the things that cause people to stumble! Such things must come, but woe to the person through who they come! If your hand or your foot causes you to stumble, cut it off and throw it away. It is better for you to enter life maimed or crippled than to have two hands or two feet and be thrown into eternal fire. And if your eye causes you to stumble, gouge it out and throw it away. It is better you enter life with one eye than to have two eyes and be thrown into the fire of hell." (Mark 9; 42-43)

There it is! There's the answer, "you (I) must change and become like a little child!" I have to change! But what does that mean? What does becoming like a child look like? What does this entail? What's its purpose? Are you telling me it's my fault? Am I responsible for what happened to me? Those were the questions stirring in my heart after reading the above verses.

I needed a few days just to let the words of Jesus in Matthew 18 settle in my spirit. When I first read the verses anger began to rise up in me. I was on the verge of letting God have it! I just kept thinking over and over again, "you have to be kidding me! I'm the one who has to change?!!!" I even looked God straight in the eyes and said, "How can you put this on me?!!!" But as time went on I started to realize that I was still caught up in the scandal of my childhood. I still believed lies about God, myself and the world. The Enemy had convinced me that the world should be perfect right now as well as everyone in it. And if it or they weren't, it was all God's fault. This world will be perfect one day, just not here and now.

I realized I was still playing the victim entitled to a personal pity party and very skilled at throwing one. But then the Holy Spirit stepped in and started to comfort me and opened my eyes to one of the most beautiful truths I had ever heard in my life; He said to me, "do not be upset, you are now going to be introduced to your new family. We have been calling out to you your whole life! We are pleased that you have heard our knock and opened the door!" Wow! It was if acceptance had finally entered my heart. Someone actually cared about me! Someone wants me to be part of their family! I get the sense I am finally going to be heard! My feelings do matter! I am not alone anymore! I also began to realize all the anger I was feeling was rising up to the surface of my heart but it was beginning to turn into praise. "Could this be the turning point for all my pain and loneliness in life?" And I believe the answer is yes!

So Papa, how do I change? And what really needs to change about me?

How do I become like a child? I believe the answers all revolved around the renewing of the mind. What is the number one characteristic of a child? They are 'believing machines!' They will believe anything you tell them and absorb it as truth. That is exactly what I must become all over again; a 'believing machine'! I must change my entire belief system from believing lies to believing truth. If I have any beliefs that cause me to stumble, they must be uprooted like weeds in a garden! I must get rid of them! That is what Jesus was talking about when he said if your eye causes you to sin pluck it out. Or if your hands and your feet cause you to sin cut them off. Get rid of the things that make you stumble; stop believing lies!

Our eye is representative of our perspective. Our foot is representative of our chosen path in life. And our hand represents the things we do (bad habits) that cause us to sin. So when Jesus says to pluck your eye out, He is saying we need to change our perspective. If we have the wrong perspective about God, ourselves, others and the world it must change to what God says is true about them. In other words to become like a child is to begin to allow God to re-parent us and teach us what is true!

So in order to be re-parented by God we must first take a look at how God regards our first parenting cycle with our earthly family. He tells us in Luke Chapter 14 what our perspective must be about how we were brought up in the world and what to do with our old belief system. Verse 26 says, "If anyone comes to me and does not hate their father and mother, wife and children, brothers and sisters-yes, even their own life-such a person cannot be my disciple. And whoever does not carry their cross and follow me cannot be my disciple." Whoa!!! What do you mean by hate my family? That was the initial thought that ran through my mind. But after spending time in prayer and studying the word 'hate' in the verse, I found that the original word used was a Greek word MISEO, which better translates to disregard, indifference, or nonattachment without any feelings. Ahhh! That makes more sense!

What Jesus was telling me was to disregard all the lies that my family, the world, the culture I grew up in and especially the Enemy had taught me as a child. God said, "Forget all the lies you were taught growing up that shaped your belief system, become like a child (believing machine) and turn to 'Me' so that I may re-parent you to know the truth and your true identity!" Wow! What a gift! I had been sensing over the past year or so that

I was being renewed in my mind and it felt like I was being re-parented, but I was unable to put it into words. A lot of what I was taught to believe as a child has caused me to stumble through life. I have now reached the point where I take a stand and can utter the words "No more stumbling!" with confidence. I am being re-parented by my heavenly family and with that will come the eradication of my old belief system.

I have also discovered that when we are caught up in the scandal of the Enemy's lies we can redefine words and pervert them as we grow older. The original meanings of words get twisted away from the truth and take on a false and misleading understanding. For example the word 'trust' meant to me, "a lower level of suspicion!" For me to trust someone was to not be one-hundred percent suspicious of them, maybe only eighty percent suspicious! Because of my stumbling I developed a motto in life that said, "Love gets you hurt, and Trust gets you killed!" That's how I defined the words love and trust. I developed this major stumbling block from two defining conversations I had with both of my parents during my high school and college years.

The first conversation took place with my mom when I was seventeen years old and a junior in high school. I had just broken up with my girlfriend and my mom decided she was going to console me with her words of wisdom and advice. She knew I was hurting and looked me straight in the eyes and said, "Listen to me, don't love just one woman; love them all! Love'em and leave'em; and when they get too close you push them away. Don't let them hurt you!" Hmmm! Ouch!!! That hit me hard and unfortunately became part of my core belief system for the better part of my life. Hence the redefinition of love; Love hurts! Now I will tell you my father's advice. It came when I was twenty-two years old and a senior in college. I found out my dad was sick with diabetes and in the hospital so I decided to drive home for a visit and go see him. I went straight to the hospital in New Jersey after an eight hour drive from school in North Carolina. I find his room and walk right in looking to cheer him up. I sat next to his bed and he started to cry! I got the sense that he felt like he was on his death bed and was about to give me my last bit of fatherly advice. So I said to him, "Pop, what's the matter?" His answer back to me went like this, "I married the wrong woman. Whatever you do don't marry the wrong woman, she will kill you!" Hmmm! Ouch again!!! That was a second core belief that has stuck with me far too long in life. "Trust will get you killed!" So with the combination of the two conversations I had with my parents, and my life perspective that was one of FEAR, I developed my new motto for life, "Love hurts and trust will get you killed!" Place that motto in your heart and you have your stumbling block for every relationship you will ever form the rest of your life; It is time to restore every word that was perverted to me as a child. It is time for truths to replace lies!

So I ask the question, "Did I interpret all that advice with the wrong perspective?" What if I had a perspective of LOVE and not FEAR? How would those messages have been received? I again sense perfect love casting out my fear. I can feel the Holy Spirit begin to pluck my blurred eye (perspective) of fear out and change it to a clear eye (perspective) of love! I begin to remember the truth that God doesn't make mistakes and He chose the two perfect people to be my parents. Then I start remembering all they did for me, even in times when they were hurting, and that's where it all turned for me! They were hurting themselves from the same kind of stumbling that they had been exposed to in their life. They weren't trying to make me stumble; they were trying to protect me! Wow!!!

That is the restoration that I have been searching for since childhood. My parents didn't want to make me stumble, they loved me! I took it wrong; I was living in my cave of fear at that time. With a new perspective of love I realize my mom was trying to protect the son that she loved so dearly. She said what she said out of her own pain but her intention was love and protection! I now hear my dad's advice as pure encouragement! He was really trying to tell me to become the man I was called to be and marry the right women; and Let God choose her! This is truly 'perfect love casting out fear!' I know my relationships are going to all change now as I move from fear to love in my perspective of life. Love makes people safe and I want to be a safe person! No more stumbling through relationships!

Let me tell you what I found out to be true about people who stumble through life; they are not safe! They are not safe people! I know I have not been a safe person but that is what I believe God is going to make me through this process of re-parenting; a safe person! To not be safe means you are stumbling through life with all of your jagged edges and battle scares received from the scandal set against you by the Enemy. An unsafe person leads with their pain and all those who come into contact with them will get slapped by their emotions before the truth be told. It is a tough and lonely way to go through life! Unsafe people tend to redefine or pervert the word passionate. They redefine emotional instability as passionate.

You tend to see this with professional athletes time and time again. You know the NFL wide receiver that has all the talent in the world but very little emotional IQ. The one that throws sideline tantrums goes off on self-centered end zone moves or can't seem to stop trash talking his opponents, teammates, coaches or anyone who doesn't bow to his talent. He's 'passionate' right? No, he is unsafe. His emotions aren't healed or balanced. He stumbles through his career, relationships and life, hurting those who dare get close to him. How do I know this to be true; that was me! I didn't have the talent to play pro football or the intestinal fortitude to not quit college football, but as a high school wide receiver I was all of the above! It cost me dearly for a large part of my life but it is restoration and re-possession time! It's time to become safe, to lead with wisdom, to not stumble, to let go of my past and all of its lies and embrace my new family and become a safe person for others to seek comfort. If I will learn to lead with wisdom my emotions will eventually catch up to the truth! Papa, please make me a safe person! Holy Spirit, teach me God's wisdom! And Jesus, please heal and restore my soul, especially my emotions!

I AM NOT ALONE

In order to heal emotionally I have to believe this: I am not alone! This is going to be the cornerstone of my changing to become like a child. I must believe that I am not an unwanted child living all alone in a dark, isolated cave anymore. I am part of a new family that loves me and accepts me as one of their own. My re-parenting will be taught by my new family: my Heavenly Father, my older brother Jesus, my counselor and good friend the Holy Spirit. Us Italians like to call him "Consigliere". I could not be in better hands!

The purpose of this re-parenting is for me to heal and restore my damaged emotions. God has been tilling the soil of my heart for a very long time now. With brokenness He has removed the 'self-will' from my heart and continues to transform my heart from a wasteland to a garden. Lies have been and are being replaced with truth. I believe it is now time to see the fruits of truth begin to produce a crop. As I have experienced restoration in my soul over the past several years: the breaking of my will and the renewing of my mind, I believe it is time for the third stage and that is the healing of my emotions. This is why I am in such need of wisdom more than ever this year. It is wisdom (the applying of the character of God (truth) to one's life) that will keep me from stumbling! It is wisdom that will restore all the damage the Enemy has inflicted to me in the garden of my heart.

This is how beautiful God's promise is regarding wisdom: Proverbs 3:21-23, "My son, do not let wisdom and understanding out of your sight, preserve sound judgement and discretion; they will be life for you, an ornament to grace your neck. Then you will go on your way in safety, and your foot will not STUMBLE!" There it is: no more stumbling!!! That's the connection between wisdom and the healing of our emotions: no more stumbling! I just can't stop repeating that phrase "no more stumbling!" It is music to my ears! The sound of freedom! I want this healing so badly I can literally begin to taste its fruit! But how do I get there? The answer is pretty clear; it is going to take another bridge crossing! And this time it will require the help of my entire new family; especially my 'Consigliere' the Holy Spirit!

REACTIONARY TO PRIMARY EMOTIONS

There she is; the 'Emotional Bridge!' It is a journey from living out of our reactionary emotions to a new life of living from our primary emotions. I am staring at this ginormous new bridge right now and I have to admit that there is no way I see myself crossing it without a guide! Here's where the Holy Spirit does some of his best work; guiding us back to the light and out of the dark recesses of our lives. In order to cross this bridge we must first have an understanding of what emotions are. Emotions are our gut feelings, sentiments, intuition and instincts. They let us know our state of mind regarding our circumstances and relationships. They tell us what we believe to be true. Emotions do not authenticate truth; they authenticate our belief of truth! So to begin this journey I must begin to feel my emotions again in order to know from where they come. I have been emotionally numb and unavailable since I was a preschooler; that's about to change!

The first lesson the Holy Spirit taught me crossing this bridge was to "learn to pause" when your emotions begin to rise! Learning to pause when you begin to feel your emotions is critical to their healing. All my life I have lived out of my 'reactionary emotions'; it was all I knew how to do. It's all one can do when living in a self-made prison of fear. They are the coping mechanisms of the cave. All one can do when they are emotional unhealthy is react to their circumstances in negative ways with reactionary emotions. Reactionary emotions are emotions such as anger, fear, worry, doubt, shame, grief, jealousy, lust, sadness, hopelessness, anxiety and guilt. Reacting out of these emotions lets you know that you are believing lies and your reactions to these lies will completely steal your joy and peace! This is why learning to pause the moment one of these emotions rises up from your gut will change your life.

Stopping that emotion and giving it to God in prayer at the moment it surfaces will allow the Holy Spirit to uncover the lie you believe. Once the Holy Spirit made me aware of 'the pause', it was as if I was thrown into a plethora of circumstances everyday which gave me opportunities to 'pause'. I soon began to catch these reactionary emotions very early and would immediately stop and ask the questions, "Where is it coming from and what lie do I believe?" Almost immediately I would hear God's voice say such things as, "pride", "entitlement" and "covetousness". "You believe a lie about 'Me'!" "You believe a lie about yourself!" "Your true identity should come from 'Me' and no one else!" Wow!!! Everything about my life began to change! I began to feel again! Stopping these emotions with a pause allowed me to feel them again, something I had been unable to do for most of my life.

After 50 years in the cold dark cave of isolation and numbness, I have begun to feel my heart again! It was just a few years ago in prayer that I cried out to God, "Papa, I am so scared!!! I have completely lost my ability to feel! Please help my heart feel again! I am terrified that it won't ever work again!" And God always answers our prayers that are noble and just and He for sure has answered my prayer to feel again! To feel again is to experience Love, Joy, Peace and Hope! Our primary emotions!

Now that we know what reactionary emotions are, it's time to find out how to move away from them and live from our God centered primary emotions. Now don't get me wrong, reactionary emotions are actually helpful. They let us know something is wrong in our thinking and believing.

We just don't want them to rule and guide our lives. The primary emotions that God gives and builds in us are love, joy, peace and hope. These are our healthy, positive emotions and are a result of accurate thoughts and beliefs. Last year's bridge from 'Behavior Modification' to 'Character Transformation' is a crucial bridge we must first cross before we can attempt to cross the emotional bridge.

You cannot just modify your behavior in life to present yourself as healthy emotionally. Jesus called those who trusted in outward behavior without true inward transformation, "white washed tombs!" That was me before I crossed the bridge from 'Behavior Modification' to 'Character Transformation'. As a 'white washed tomb' myself I had come to this conclusion; "I must find a way to survive this life and make it look good until I get to heaven!" But that is an unproductive life and I just couldn't fake it anymore. My desire is now to be a hundred fold producer and in order to produce a crop and bear fruit like love, joy, peace, patience, kindness, goodness, faith, meekness and self-control; you must allow God to transform you inwardly by the healing of your emotions.

So what is God's purpose in moving us from living out of our reactionary emotions to living from our primary ones; Emotional Maturity! That is what this stage of the restoring of our soul is going to do; restore us to emotional maturity in order to handle the God given purpose of our lives! So I ask the question; what is the goal of emotional maturity? The answer is "To act our age!" especially when something distressful happens. By giving us wisdom and healing us emotionally, God is teaching us to live from the heart that Jesus gave us!

The apostle Paul said it best, "When I was a child, I talked like a child, I thought like a child, I reasoned like a child. When I became a man (a mature, healthy emotional adult), I put those the ways of childhood behind me." God is re-parenting me to maturity. Emotional healing is my right of passage to adulthood! In this process I am learning to rest more in the garden. I am realizing I can't go it alone anymore in life, I need a helper. I am learning that love does not have to hurt and trust won't get you killed if directed by God. When you are in the child stage of emotions; one's self is enough! But as an emotional healthy adult, relationship with others is the way to go! I am no longer alone internally and I don't think I will be alone much longer outwardly!

Crossing the bridge from 'Reactionary Emotions' to 'Primary Emotions' will require a few things; the ability to forgive and to trust! Two things an unsafe emotionally unhealthy child of God lacks. It is almost impossible to forgive and trust others when reactionary emotions are ruling your life. I cannot wait to taste the freedom that comes with living from primary emotions!

ART OF FORGIVENESS AND TRUSTING

Trust is the pathway into life and the foundation of our personal relationships! Life literally begins with trust. Without trust we are dead while we are literally living! God has made it very clear to me that if I am going to live in the garden as a mature emotional healthy adult child of God; I am going to have to learn to trust. Trust is a crucial issue inside the garden! Maturing as a child of God is learning how to actively trust. Trust and love are the basis of all healthy relationships; hence, the critical importance of last year's quest to love. Love is now being coupled with learning to trust (emotional maturity) and the foundation of life in the garden is being established. Emotions are the music of the soul! If we have a solid foundation of love and trust, the music will sound like love, joy, peace and hope; music to my ears! Love and trust are the relational vehicles that allow God to get involved in our lives. Therefore, trust is critical to our spiritual growth.

It was recently shared with me that "true intimacy comes from resolved conflict!" Let that one seep deep down into the garden of your heart! Now if that is true and I believe that it is, then we must learn the art of forgiveness! If my motto in life has been, "Love hurts and trust will get you killed", there is no chance for me to live as that emotionally mature adult in this world. My motto must change; it must be restored to one that agrees with what God says about love and trust. Without trust conflicts will never be solved and therefore intimacy will never be experienced. Remember the bridge from a 'Mocker' to a 'Lover', "Drive out the mocker and out goes strife; quarrels and insults are ended." Mockers don't trust; they are skeptical and suspicious. But lovers have learned to trust; Trusting means to have a firm belief in the reliability, ability or strength of someone and to place confidence in them. If I am going to walk in love I will have to begin to trust people again. No more retreating to my dark lonely cave of isolation every time I feel threatened or vulnerable. I am going to have to participate in life and that requires trust.

Without trust there is no relationship. Therefore without trust one will be alone for the rest of their life even if they are in relationships of all kinds. There will never be a connection, a deep intimate one; just surface connections that can break as easily as cheap glass. I now can see the importance of the many bridges I have crossed that have lead me to this point of re-establishing trust in my heart. A person with trust in their heart has the ability to forgive. They can overlook the offense of another and know it comes from their pain and ultimately the Evil one. And probably the greatest person of all that I need to forgive is myself. It's not all my fault. I didn't ask to be mistreated or abandoned emotionally a child.

I never wanted to live in that dark, lonely cave. I went there to survive because I was afraid. It's okay now to walk out of the cave and begin to live because I have a new loving family to walk it out with me. I will learn to trust and forgive with each new step I take in the garden. It is becoming a safe place for me and will make me a safe person to be with. I know I have not been safe to be with most of my life. I lived most of my life out of my reactionary emotions, they were my defense and coping mechanisms. I didn't want to hurt or abandon anyone, I was just too afraid of relationships because they required trust; something I believed would get me killed! But I know it doesn't have to be that way anymore. I have to believe in the process thus far! All the trauma, adversity, disappointment, loss, suffering, abandonments, conflicts, trials and pain were orchestrated by God to get me to where I am today. The Enemy may have tried to steal my maturity and dreams; but my 'Papa' is a God of restoration, reconciliation and redemption. By having my emotions healed, trust restored and love redefined, I will walk into my future with the confidence that I will not only survive but thrive!

In order to learn the art of forgiveness one has to look no further than 1st Corinthians chapter 13, "Love… it keeps no record of wrongs!" The quest to love is still going strong! There it is! If I am going to be a lover I will keep no record of wrongs, past, present or future. I will forgive them all; especially those of my parents who loved me with all their heart. No more harboring ill will because someone acted out of pain and hurt my feelings.

It's time to grow up and let bygones be bygones! I'm starting to get that loving feeling again and it feels like maturity!

THE DAY MATURITY SET IN

What seemed to be just another commute to work on the morning of June 1, 2016, turned into one of the coolest revelations I have ever experienced from God. It may defy logic but I can honestly say that my perspective of who I am changed in an instant – in a moment I had gone from being a boy to becoming a man. Let me explain!

While driving and listening to a sermon about wanting God's best in life a wave of peace came over me like a tidal wave and consumed me. It felt like my entire disposition had instantly changed. At that moment I remember uttering these words to myself out loud, "I'm feeling mature!" I may never be fully able to explain that, but it's what I felt. I remember looking at my left hand on the steering wheel and it was just resting on it very gently. I was no longer gripping the wheel with both hands tightly fisted. My grip had changed from one of a white knuckled tight tension hold to simply RESTING on the wheel! It was if I finally put my **TRUST** in God and what He says is true about me, as well as the work He has done in me!

I still can't truly explain the feeling, but it was as if the way I would look at myself for the rest of my life had just changed. I was no longer going to perceive myself as that scared little boy hiding in a dark lonely cave trying to survive in a tough adult world. My perspective of myself had changed. I had my eye plucked out! I began to realize that if I was going to walk out this journey as an emotionally mature adult I could no longer see myself as a scared little boy. **We cannot perceive ourselves one way and live another; it won't work!** That's what the purpose of the bridge from 'Behavior Modification' to 'Character Transformation' is all about; no more faking it!

So as I sense my perspective about myself begin to change and be restored to its original state of maturity expressing itself with primary emotions, I believe my perspective about God is also changing. It has gone from one of suspicion to one of trust. I finally reached a point in my journey where I would put my trust in God wholeheartedly. My perspective of God had changed. He began to feel safe to me. And putting my trust in Him just felt safe to do as well. Maybe if I can put my trust in God I can begin to trust others as well. We will see what the future holds.

So now I feel as if I am being lead toward another bridge to help me better understand my past as well as my new perspective. I have a sense that this bridge will be different than any of the previous bridges I have crossed!

RAGGEDY SNEAKERS

I believe that in order to fully mature emotionally we have to let go of our past. It is that part of the restoration process that helps us disregard what our family and society taught us about ourselves growing up. All of us have dealt with some adversity as a child, some more than others, but growing up in a home that is filled with ongoing daily adversity that causes constant stress can and will typically rear its ugly head in adulthood. Researchers and physicians over the past twenty years have begun to find and see a correlation between childhood adversity and onset adult diseases such as cancer, heart disease and auto immune diseases. I am beginning to believe this is true. Let me give you an example of this; me! As I have stated before about my childhood I feel I was mistreated emotionally, mentally, verbally and spiritually.

The constant barrage of condemnation and negativity I experienced as a child drove me to my cave around the age of three where I sat there in fear and loneliness for the better part of my life up until now. I have one very distinct memory that illustrates this point. It was the day I was going to take my first physical so I could play Pop Warner football. I was seven or eight years old at that time. All of the potential players who signed up for the team would have to meet at one physician's office at the same time so we could get our physicals. It is supposed to be a fun time to meet the other kids and begin a new chapter of life playing organized sports. Now after all the kids had arrived we formed a line and waited our turns to get the okay to play. I am standing about halfway through the line and I watch every kid in front of me go through the few tests they had that collected data like height and weight. They also would check your eyes, ears, heart and test for blood pressure. This all looked simple enough till it reached my turn and the doctor wrapped the blood pressure kit around my arm.

Here is where my childhood fear of death and disease started to take root in my heart. I remember the Doctor saying "Hmmmm!!! "What do you mean by hmmmm?!" went through my mind. "You didn't say that to any of the other kids!" The next thing I heard was the doctor say to my mom, "Have him go sit outside alone for a bit and see if he can calm down! His blood pressure is quite high. We'll try him again later". So my mom took me outside to a bench to sit me down alone to calm my nerves. Sure! Great idea! Isolation is the answer! That will help a eight year old scared to death that there is something physically wrong calm down. That was the same lie Satan sold me when I was three! Go sit in your lonely isolated dark cave with all your fears and I will come tend to them and cause them to grow in your life; you will be safe from others! Breaking news alert! **"Isolation doesn't calm your fears it expands them!"**

I don't think my mom, the doctor or the world knew what I was going through at that moment; but God did! And that's why He re-parents those that are willing to learn and become like little children again! Believe it or not I can still picture the entire scene where I sat alone outside the doctor's office to this day. I was wearing shorts, a t-shirt and a raggedy old pair of sneakers. How do I know that they were raggedy old sneakers? Because I distinctly remember sitting on that old wooden bench staring down at the ground watching my own two little feet in those raggedy sneakers swing back and forth under me as I sat there in complete fear and isolation!

The conversation in my head went something like this, "Why me? None of the others kids had anything wrong with them. Why am I the only one sick? Why can't I just be like the other kids? I thought high blood pressure was for grown-ups? This doesn't make any sense! Am I being punished? What did I do wrong? See! Here I am again all alone; I don't belong with the others. I just need to go to my cave where I belong and am safe, right?" I don't want those memories to run my adult life anymore. They are literally killing me! "Papa, help me to walk into the future without carrying all that baggage. I just want to leave it in the cave and walk away from it forever; how do I do that?" The answer; "It's time to cross another bridge my son!"

FROM BIOGRAPHY TO BIOLOGY

And there it was right in front of me, a brand new bridge and it's called from 'Biography' to 'Biology'! This is the bridge that deals with childhood trauma and its physical affects in adulthood. But it is very different from the many bridges I have crossed. As I stare at it I see that it is quite dim and has the word 'Shame' above it. Not only can I see the word shame, but I can hear it; those words I heard hundreds of times as a child, "Shame on you" were gently being whispered in my ear as I stood there contemplating my entrance onto this bridge.

My childhood was absolutely a shame based childhood. In my mind it has resulted in me living in a constant state of anxiety as well as having a plethora of physical diseases that are wreaking havoc on my body. My own personal study of adverse childhood experiences and their link to adult chronic diseases leads me to believe this is true. Here's the current list of my conditions plaguing my health. I have been coughing chronically now for three years and the doctors have no clue as to what is causing it. They think it has to do with a combination of my persistent acid reflux (auto-immune), allergies (which I have too many to count) and Sarcoidosis, a lymph node infection in my lung (auto-immune). Let's not forget that I have Raynaud's disease, a vascular disorder (auto immune) and on and off high blood pressure. I also had my arthritic right hip totally replaced this year, just letting you know about that one for kicks! To be honest it is physically brutal in my life right now and it is God's grace alone that gets me through every day. It is my new found hope I discovered a few years ago that over rides my physical struggles. It's also the belief that this bridge I am about to cross is going to address a lot of what ails me.

Now as God continues to re-parent, my trust in Him to know what is best keeps getting tested in order for it to grow. I can hear him say to me, "I know your path on this bridge seems dark, but trust me to walk you through it; your new family will be your guide!" As scared as I am I know I don't really have a choice to cross this bridge or not because the only other option besides crossing it is physical death. So here we go, God, the Holy Spirit, Jesus, myself and a few good friends: all together we begin our journey across this bridge. As we begin walking out this part of my journey over this bridge more and more painful childhood memories surface, along with their deep rooted lies. God assures me, "That's not who you are! That is a lie from the Enemy!" Then He counteracts it with, "The truth is 'I Love You!' You are my child and I only have good things in store for you! Trust me and let go of your past!"

After years of trying to get me to this point in my life where I trust in Him enough to let go of the pain of my past, I finally get far enough along this bridge to see a sign ahead that reads "EXIT NOW!" "What …? An exit ramp on a bridge! I have never seen one of them before! Not only was this sign surprising, it was also quite unnerving and seemed to lead to darkness! Can there be an exit ramp in the middle of a bridge? I mean the sign "EXIT NOW" was lit up and crystal clear to me that this was my exit. I had a sense that this exit ramp was here specifically for me. Here is where three good friends of mine all spoke words of encouragement to me (confirmation) months before I knew of this bridge. It was if they were prophesying my future journey on this bridge. They all said in separate conversations that it was time for me to let go of my past and not let it define who I was anymore. It was time for the truth to grow in my heart and I needed desperately to let go of my childhood biography (my past) before it destroyed my adult biology (my physical and emotional health). It was time to take the exit ramp that seemed to lead to darkness but in reality was the way to God's light.

So let me be honest, I was scared! That exit ramp to God's light looked like the entrance to a hole in the universe that drops off into perpetual darkness. And I believe the Enemy wants it to appear that way when in reality this the greatest exits one could take. He doesn't want anyone to take this exit because He'll no longer be able to control them (me) with His fear. But again for me the choice is simple, not easy, but simple; exit now or die prematurely from disease! So to help me choose to exit this bridge God spoke to me words from the prophet Isaiah. God knows how afraid we can be of darkness and the unknown that it brings! It takes a lot of courage and encouragement to take this exit and change your life. So as I prepare to exit I hear the words of Isaiah whispered in my ear, "I will give you the treasures of darkness, riches stored in secret places, so that you may know that I am the Lord, the God of Israel, who summons you by name." (Isaiah 45:3) Wow! There are treasures in darkness? What does that mean?

Then I remembered a good friend of mine shared this verse with me through a book he wrote in April 1996. I never understood the meaning of that verse till now. We go through some dark times in life in order to find the light. This verse is just now beginning to bear fruit in my life. God spent twenty years to get me prepared to exit this bridge. But God is love and "Love always perseveres!" Again, learning another aspect of love! It took twenty years of trials, hardships and discipline to build my trust in Him so I could choose the exit ramp off this bridge. In August of 1996, four months after my friend shared Isaiah 45:3 with me, I was shown Isaiah 45:7, which introduced me to the truth that God is in control of all things good or bad. "I form the light and create darkness. I bring prosperity and create disaster. I, the Lord, do all these things" Remembering this verse now helps give me the courage to walk through dark times in life and gives me the courage to take what seems to be this dark exit off this bridge. If God created this exit, no matter how scary it looks to me, it must be for my good. I have to trust that God is in control and this exit ramp is in my best interest. So finally at the age of fifty-one I have mustered up enough strength, courage and trust in God to exit this bridge. I'm turning off and saying goodbye to my past of fear and lies!

In choosing to take the exit off the bridge from 'Biography' to 'Biology' I believe I have taken another major step in the development of my emotional IQ. Choosing to walk on this bridge under the entrance sign of 'Shame' was a huge step. To exit off this bridge into the darkness of the unknown is another huge step. They are major steps in letting go of the fears that have plagued my life since childhood. And just as God had prepared my heart for such a time as this through the words of Isaiah the prophet twenty years ago, it is through Isaiah's words again that He comforts me as I turn to take the exit off this bridge. God gently whispers in my ear, "Do not be afraid; you will not suffer **shame.** Do not fear disgrace; you will not be humiliated. **YOU WILL FORGET THE SHAME OF YOUR YOUTH…**" (Isaiah 54:4) I am just sitting here with Jesus and the Holy Spirit in amazement; just me not them. What a promise! Oh, to walk away from the shame of my youth and not to have to experience it daily; "Everything is possible for him who believes." (Mark 9:23)" My responsibility in this journey now becomes even clearer to me; believe! So I cry out to God with the words from (Mark 9:24), "I do believe; help me overcome my unbelief!" Now that I have chosen to exit this bridge; what now Papa? God says, "Believe that I have your back!"

GOD HAS MY BACK, RIGHT?

As I walk down the exit ramp I ask the question, "Do I really believe that God has my back?" To me it's not a quick or simple yes or no answer. It is one that I must sit and meditate on, which I did for quite a bit this year. Over the past year and a half I was lead to read Psalm 91 every single day. I felt like it was medicine to my soul to help me eradicate many illegitimate and legitimate fears. Verses 1 and 2 are statement verses which read, "He who dwells in the shelter of the most high will **rest** in the shadow of the Almighty. I will say of the Lord, "He is my refuge and my fortress, my God, in whom I trust."" Do I believe that to be true? Am I dwelling in His shelter and resting in His shadows? Do I really trust Him? Do I believe God has my back? Because if I do believe that God has my back everything will change. So just in curiosity I look up the definition of 'got your back' and it reads like this, "A person saying they have **your back** means they are there to help you out, they will watch out and take care of the things you're likely to miss, that they are a second set of eyes and hands for you." Wow! So believing that God has my back is truly an act of faith. It is the act of putting my trust in Him that no matter what happens, that He is right there with me watching over me through it all!

Believing God has my back is the pathway to relationship and healing. It is necessary in that it helps us continue our journey to the garden through dark times. Back in 2013 I told of how God wanted to deliver me from the fear of man which proved to be a snare in life. He exposed me to (Hebrews 13:5-6), "Never will I leave you; never will I forsake you." So we say with confidence, "The Lord is my helper; I will not be afraid. What can man do to me?" God planted that truth in the garden of my heart over three years ago and my believing that God has my back is the fruit that will blossom from that truth.

Believing that God has my back will also allow me to be vulnerable, which we know is profoundly important to experiencing the life God has planned for us. I also believe now that if I don't believe that God has my back, cynicism will begin to creep back into the garden of my heart. I will begin to take back perceived control of the steering wheel with the tight grip and bust out all the coping mechanisms I used to fake my way through life. I will live life again with the attitude that it all depends on me and I have to watch out for myself; I have to have my own back! To believe that God does not have my back points me in the direction of my dark isolated cave, the place I never want to go again.

So how do I go from not believing God has my back to believing that God does? To believe that God has my back requires I cross another bridge and it's the one I see at the bottom of the exit ramp. It's a small one that is built to cross the waters beneath the bridge I just exited. It is a tiny little bridge at the end of the exit ramp called from 'I got this' to 'God's got this!' It might be a very small and short bridge, but it is one that will leave a marker stating, "No matter what happens, from now on, God has my back!"

Let me sum up the journey thus far on the bridge from 'Biography' to 'Biology'. This is a bridge from Biography (our childhood experiences/good and bad) to Biology (our adult state of mental and physical health). First, in order for God to re-parent us, we must let go of our past. And to let go of our past we must first accept that it happened. That is taking ownership of our past, and only in doing so can we finally let it go and give it to God. My past happened to me and there is nothing I can do about it now except own it and let it go! By letting go of the past and exiting this bridge I can now become like a little child again, 'a believing machine', and let God teach me the truth about who I am as opposed to the Enemy filling my heart with lies that lead to fear and condemnation. Letting go of the past will also give me the courage to trust God with my future and believe that He truly does have my back. This will then allow me to live life with the vulnerability that it requires. Relationships will become safe, I will become safe and God will be able to place things in my life that He was never able to because they would have been rejected, manipulated, destroyed or broken!

Now after choosing the seemingly dark exit ramp off the 'Biography to Biology' bridge that lead me to a little bridge below it called from 'I got this' to 'God's got this' I find myself on the other side of the bridge staring at an entrance ramp! This entrance is brightly lit up and reads; 'Love's Way!' The thoughts in my mind are going crazy right now! What is going on here? I just got off this bridge! Then it hits me; we are switching sides! This is my chance to get back on the bridge, but this time on the side of love not shame! The Holy Spirit gently whispers in my ear," This is the way to go! Take it!" And I do. I am running up this ramp like the police are chasing me. I can't wait to get back on the bridge away from the darkness of the exit ramp and clear from the water beneath to high ground where there is light, warmth and safety. It's the 'Love' side of the bridge and I am on it headed to my new future!

As I begin walking, it suddenly hits me and I look at the Holy Spirit with this huge smile and say, "Now I get it; Water under the Bridge!!!" I finally realize what that saying truly means when people say it! To say that something is water under the bridge means that you've let it go! It's over! It's behind you! I finally get to say that about my past, "its water under the bridge!" Are you kidding me?! Did you just follow the journey Papa took me on to let go of my shame ridden past and set me on a course of Love for my future! Who does that but God!!! That's restoration at its finest!

For twenty years God prepared my heart to eventually reach the point where I could trust Him to introduce me to a bridge that will change my past, present and future. He started me out taking the path of shame only to convince me to leave that path and exit down a dark ramp that lead to another small bridge I needed to cross over the waters of my shameful past that eventually lead me to the other side of the bridge that was lit up and covered with love. It was a crazy, up and down, zig zag way to go, but it worked. I can now look back to my crazy shame filled past and say, "Its water under the bridge!" I am free to walk in Love and let God re-parent me with the truth of who I truly am. I cannot wait to see what the garden of my heart will look like as my thoughts about myself begin to change with love. I believe that my garden is about to bloom like flowers in springtime! I feel the need to put on a pair of sunglasses because hope tells me that regardless of my past, my future is bright now that I believe God has my back and we are walking on the path of love! Papa, thank you for re-parenting me!

> **"When a train goes through a tunnel and it gets dark,**
> **you don't throw away the ticket and jump off. YOU**
> **SIT AND TRUST THE ENGINEER."**
> **- Corrie Ten Boom -**

REVENANT

Earlier this year I watched a movie called "The Revenant". I was warned by a few people that although they thought it was a good movie, they felt its overall theme was one of darkness. That kind of reminded me of how I would describe my own past. I decided to watch it anyway and found that my heart was quickly captured by what I thought its overall theme to be; one that I would describe as "perseverance!" What the world often sees as darkness God sees as the development of our faith through perseverance. Perseverance is the character trait that will enable a child of God who has learned to hear God's word and retain it in his soul to finish the course God has set for their life. If you want to be a hundred fold producer for the kingdom of God, you must be able to persevere through whatever trial or obstacle God places before you on your path to the garden. Let's take a look at the journey of the main character of The Revenant 'Hugh Glass'.

Hugh Glass was a frontiersman who was hired by a fur trading company to guide their trappers through the wilderness in order to trap and collect valuable furs to be sold for large profits. He was married to a Native-American woman who had been murdered by Federal troops in one of their raids. He managed to escape that raid along with his one and only son. After being hired, along with his son by the fur trading company they were again attacked by a tribe of Native-Americans only to escape with just a few men and a few fur pelts. Most of the fur traders were killed and their furs stolen. After him, his son and the other men managed their escape they found themselves hungry and alone in the middle of the wilderness far away from their base camp. So Hugh, being the guide that he was, decided to go hunting alone to get some meat for his hungry companions while they rested at a makeshift camp. It was then that he was blindsided and attacked by a bear defending her cubs. Hugh eventually killed the bear after a long and torturous bout with its powerful teeth and claws. The attack left him with many broken bones as well as a slash to the throat which had him gasping for his final breaths. His men soon found him after hearing the shot that killed the bear, but their initial response after seeing his mangled body was that it was only a matter of time before Hugh would succumb to his wounds.

The other men tried to carry Hugh back to camp through the wilderness but it had become futile because of the snowy terrain and cold. They had no choice but to leave Hugh behind to die. Two men plus his son were then given the task to stay behind and wait out Hugh's last days together and then give him a proper burial. But after a day or so one of the men, Fitzgerald, who we would soon learn to be Hugh's biggest nemesis, was no longer willing to wait for Hugh to die and take the risk of being attacked by Native-Americans. So he decided to take matters into his own hands. In short, he ended up killing Hugh's son while Hugh watched unable to speak or move, therefore erasing the only witness to his evil plan. Then Fitzgerald, through his tactic of fear and deception convinced the last man who was away gathering water to abandon Hugh while still alive and head back to camp before they themselves would be killed by those who were tracking them. So there lays Hugh in a pile of dirt, covered with snow, broken bones and numerous open wounds, including the slashed throat that robbed him of his voice, along with the vision of his son being murdered; what should he do? What would you do? What would I do?

Let's be honest, most everyone alive would hope to die and get it over quickly. His chances of recovery were slim at best and the pain to make it out alive was going to be unbearable! In my dark past where I found myself in the same situation (metaphorically), I wondered if it would just be best if the Lord took me back home so that the pain and struggle of life would finally end! I felt like giving up so many times. Questions like, "Why fight to live if the future will be like the past?" would go through my mind! They are times of despair every child of God will go through, but to succumb to quitting and giving up I believe will cause those who do so to miss out on God's blessing. But for those who choose to persevere, they will get the chance to wear the crown given by heaven for their faith. The writer of the book of Hebrews puts it best (Hebrews 10: 35-39), "So do not throw away your confidence; it will be richly rewarded. You need to **persevere** so that when you have done the will of God, you will receive what He has promised. For in a very little while, "He who is coming will come and will not delay. But my righteous one will live by faith. And if he shrinks back, I will not be pleased with him." But we are not those who shrink back and are destroyed, but of those who believe and are saved."

Hugh Glass never gave up. He crawled out of that pile of dirt and started one of the most incredible journeys of determination one will ever watch, read or hear about. Hugh persevered through several encounters with those who pursued him to take his life as well as some of the harshest weather conditions; along with eating anything and everything possible to reach his final destination which was base camp. And after one of the most amazing feats of perseverance imaginable, he was finally found by his men and taken back to camp; Hugh had persevered! When he finally arrived there he had discovered that the man, his nemesis Fitzgerald, who left him for dead after killing his son, was there but had now disappeared into the woods for fear the truth would finally expose his deeds. Now Hugh, after just barely making it back to camp, regrouped and headed back out to find his nemesis and deal with him once and for all. Hugh eventually found Fitzgerald and after a tough struggle with hand to hand combat was finally able to subdue him and sent him floating down a stream into the hands of a war party that killed him. So not only did Hugh Glass persevere through some of the most difficult and tumultuous experiences anyone would ever face, he finished the journey by subduing his enemy and moved on to his future with his life intact; battered and bruised, but intact. The movie doesn't tell you about the rest of Hugh's life; it just shared his struggle to survive the ultimate test of perseverance. But we as believers have been told what the future will be for those who persevere; and it is good!

My journey thus far has made me feel as if I too am 'The Revenant', Definition; A person who has returned, especially supposedly from the dead! From the day my will was broken in January of 2010, and even several years before, I felt as if I too have been raked over the coals seventy-seven times! I have laid face down on the floor, sat in the corner of a room, laid in a hospital bed, driven hundreds of thousands of miles, rested on the shoreline of the ocean, sat on the edge of a bay, stared at the heavens on the peak of a mountain, walked through desserts and valleys and all of this I have done wondering if I was ever going to make it out of the cave of darkness and isolation I was imprisoned in all my life! Every time I thought I had finally become free, something, some trial, some test or some tragedy would knock me down again and send me retreating back to my cave for safety. But ever since brokenness occurred in my life, every test of perseverance would now make me just a little bit stronger! In my pre-broken state of life, tests of perseverance would weaken me rather than strengthen me; But not anymore.

Brokenness is the gift of God that allows you to persevere under trial! Perseverance is what strengthens the root system of our gardens. Here is a quote from the Revenant that appeared on screen while Hugh Glass was struggling through the wilderness to survive; "The wind cannot defeat a tree with strong roots. When there is a storm… and you stand in front of a tree… If you look at its branches, you swear it will fall. But if you watch the trunk you will see its **stability**." Perseverance sends our roots deep down into the soil of our gardens. It's what gives us stability in times of testing from the storms of life. I have said it before and will say it again; Brokenness, no matter how painful, is a gift from God, especially when it comes to developing perseverance!

So what is God's ultimate purpose in putting a child of His through so many almost unbearable trials; Productivity! (2nd Peter 1:5-9), "For this very reason, make every effort to add to your faith goodness; and to goodness, knowledge; and to knowledge, self-control; and to self-control, **perseverance**; and to perseverance, godliness; and to godliness, mutual affection; and to mutual affection, love. For if you possess these qualities in increasing measure, they will **keep you from being ineffective and unproductive** in your knowledge of our Lord Jesus Christ. But whoever does not have them is nearsighted and blind, forgetting that **they have been cleansed from their past sins."** This verse demonstrates both the importance of persevering and the crossing the previous bridge from 'Biography' to 'Biology' in order to let go of your past!

Watching Hugh Glass persevere through the many life threatening, heart breaking and anguishing tests and trials he went through gave me hope! I didn't see this movie as darkness, I saw it as light shining through the darkness; I saw it as perseverance! Why did I see it that way you might ask? Because God says, "Consider it pure joy, my brothers, whenever you face trials of many kinds, because you know that the testing of your faith develops perseverance. Perseverance must finish its work so that you may be mature and complete, not lacking anything." (James 1:2-4). If you want to become a hundredfold producer in the kingdom of God you must be able to persevere through all that life will throw at you!

During Hugh's darkest moments of his journey to make it out of the wilderness alive he would often remember lessons of his past and through visualizing these memories he would find the strength to carry on. In one scene he is remembering the time his wife was murdered and he was consoling his son to persevere through this moment of devastation. His conversation to his son was now the memory that would help him to persevere. The words from that conversation were subtitled on the screen and read like this, **"It's okay son... I know you want this to be over. I'm right here. I will be right here... But, you don't give up. You hear me? As long as you can still grab a breath, you fight. You breathe... keep breathing."**

Those are some comforting words from a father to a son in times of testing. And they are the exact words our Heavenly father speaks to us in our times of distress and darkness. He knows what's at stake. He knows the end is good for those who persevere and that He will not be pleased with those who shrink back and give up. Although many of my struggles were physical, most of my pain came from my emotional battles. Though it will take some time, most of our physical wounds will heal relatively quick compared to the healing of our emotional wounds. Emotional wounds are deep in our soul, much deeper that our physical wounds which are on the surface. Perseverance will allow God to go deep in our soul and heal!

CHANGING THE SOIL

In order to heal emotionally we need to allow God to go deep into our soul and do what only He can do. What I believe God is doing when He goes deep into our soul for emotional healing is change the soil of our garden! I often wondered if it was possible to change the soil of one's garden; their soul. I'm now certain that it is possible. I think of the parable of the Sower. The farmer in the parable was scattering seed to produce a crop and there were four different kinds of soil; (1) hard soil along the path - people who refuse to hear the word of God. (2) shallow soil mixed with rock - people who hear the word of God but don't have the root system to retain it and will produce nothing. (3) soil with thorns - people who hear the word of God but the lies of the world choke it out and they shrink back and give up, and (4) **good** soil! This soil will produce a crop- thirty, sixty or a hundred times what was sown. So I continue to ask the question; can the soil of our heart change? The answer is YES!

If I were to be honest with you I would say that when I started this journey of brokenness my heart was one of good soil, but my life was filled with many weeds. My soul was a garden of good soil overrun by thorns, thistles and weeds. My garden became a wasteland through lies! But it has changed and is changing still. God has been pulling weeds and planting truth in my heart ever since brokenness occurred. When I decided to leave the wasteland through the door of hope and cross the 'Bridge of Brokenness' (Galatians 2:20) and enter God's rest and journey to the garden, God's restoration process of my soul went into heaven's speed! His perfect love began casting out all the lies and fears the Enemy had sown in the soil of my heart since I was a child. But to remove the weeds (lies) from our gardens in just the first step in restoration. The second step was to strengthen the soil and turn it into good clean soil, to till or prepare the soil for production. The next step is to plant seed in order to produce a crop, preferably a hundred times what is sown!

SOIL NEEDS SEED

If my heart and soul have been changed from a wasteland to a garden, what will it take to produce a crop? And not just any crop, a hundred fold crop!

Earlier in this journey I talked about wanting God's best. And in order to receive God's best you have to become God's best; the person He intended you to be! I believe that God's best for our lives is to be a hundred fold producer. We've seen on this journey the process of brokenness and the amazing changes that will occur to the gardens of our souls when it is allowed to complete its work. The soil of our garden or heart can actually be changed for the better. But once the soil has become good and ready for crop production I believe it will need seed to produce a crop.

Early on in my journey of brokenness I was introduced to a verse that would change everything about my life. A verse that states how life can come only from death to self, and produce the abundant life we as children of God are promised. It is John 12:24 "Very truly I tell you, unless a kernel of wheat falls to the ground and dies, it remains only a single seed. But if it dies, it produces many seeds." This verse appears for a second time in this journey, but this time it focuses on the multiplication of the seed! What is necessary to produce a hundred fold crop? What is necessary to receive Gods best in this life? After walking out this journey of brokenness for the past six years this is what I have discovered; a handful of eight principles (seeds) to be scattered among our gardens in order to produce a hundred fold crop!

I was taught these eight principles from a mentor I have never met, Derek Prince, but have listened to for hundreds of hours while driving over the past decade or so. I am forever grateful! Here are the eight seeds I believe must become part of our lives, our gardens and our souls if we are going to produce a hundred fold crop and receive Gods best for our lives. (1) Want God's best! This isn't just a truism. It is the absolute starting point and non-negotiable principle to receiving God's best; you must want God's best above all else and be resolved to not settle for anything less! (2) Focus on Jesus! Remember; your focus becomes your reality! (3) Meditate in God's word! Saturate your mind with His Word so that in infiltrates every thought and consumes your thinking! (4) Make friends with the Holy Spirit! He is the perfect guide for this journey, better than any GPS system humanity can create! (5) Hear and obey God's Word promptly! This is lesson #1 that we learn on our journey to the garden! That should say it all! (6) Be careful how and what you here! This is lesson number #1A in the garden; stop listening to strange voices! Let God be the protector of the ear gate of your garden's boundaries! (7) Be more concerned with the Eternal than the Temporal! Ecclesiastes 3:11 says, "… He (God) has also set eternity in the human heart…" (8) Let God choose for you! Let God choose your inheritance! Let him choose what you will receive and produce! "A person can receive only what is given them from heaven. (John 3:27)" Here is what I know for sure; God gives His best to those who let Him choose!

If we will let these eight principles guide our journey, they will sow many seeds and will produce a crop a hundred times what was sown! Think again about what is necessary to produce a crop; Luke 8:15 "But the seed on good soil stands for those with a noble and good heart, who hear the word, retain it and by persevering produce a good crop." It takes good soil to produce a hundred fold crop and emotional health is a sign of good soil!

MAKING THE TURN HOME

As this year comes to a close I am reminded of the many lessons I have been taught, the many bridges I crossed and the many promises I have been given thus far in my journey. So many of them are now established or being established in my garden and are beginning to bear fruit. God first promised to restore all things, which includes healing them, establishing them, repossessing them, and making them fruitful. His promises are true and the garden of my heart is experiencing those truths and is becoming more and more an example of God's love. This year saw my garden find a new and much larger place with new soil and the opportunity for so much new growth in Gainesville, GA.

I am reminded of when God told me I was root-bound and needed a new home and new soil in order to grow. That He would have to uproot me and put me in a temporary place (Wrightsville Beach) so that my roots could get healthy enough to be placed in a new and larger place. He brought me back to Atlanta with the promise that he would then establish me. Little did I know that He had a small town in the North Georgia Mountains all prepared for me. It is a place that feels like home already; somewhere where I feel like putting down some roots! This entire journey that I have been on truly feels like a journey from a wasteland existence to life in a garden. Everything is different in my life except that I am still single, but that singleness is now very different as well.

As I think about the journey, I ask myself; how did it happen? I know it came about by God answering my prayers to get out of the prison I was living in, but how was He able to get me from point A to point B so many times and in so many ways? The answer is crystal clear; by listening to the voice of God and God alone! Learning to hear the voice of God is the only way the Holy Spirit can guide us on this journey. Without the ability to hear God's voice you will be spiritually malnourished. Learning to hear the voice of God requires sitting alone with Him and meditating on His word; no way around it! It takes time and effort; there are no shortcuts to this process.

Up to this point in my journey I have awoken at 6:00 am almost every day to spend at least an hour with God; praying, studying and listening. For me, there is no sweeter song that can compare to the voice of God whispered in your ear as you spend time with Him. It is the prize given to those who are willing to put their relationship with God first and foremost before anything else in this world. So if you haven't already learned to hear His voice I suggest that you do whatever it takes to make that the priority of your life. It is the very first lesson we are commanded to learn when we enter God's rest and begin our journey home. It is the number one characteristic of a hundred fold producer in the garden.

My initial prayer this year was to receive the wisdom necessary to develop emotionally and become a hundred fold producer in the kingdom of God. It is best prayed the way King Solomon prayed in 1st Kings 3:9, "So give your servant a discerning heart to govern your people and to distinguish between right and wrong..." And if your prayer is as sincere as Solomon's I believe you will hear the voice of God respond from proverbs 4:20-21 with His answer, "My son pay attention (Listen) to what I say; turn your ear to my words. Do not let them out of your sight, keep them within your heart." In others words, get in God's word and listen to what He has to say and let His words be established in your heart!

Am I there yet? A hundred fold producer? Probably not. But my heart tells me I am on the path with still many tests and trials to go. It won't be easy but the tools are being developed and the root system is starting to establish itself deeper and deeper. Again my prayer to begin this year was to obtain wisdom, discernment and emotional health to continue the journey. My prayer to end this year is one of protection from falling away and becoming unproductive. The prophet Amos states it this way in (8:11) "The days are coming," declares the Lord, when I will send a famine through the land - not a famine of food or a thirst for water, but a famine of hearing the words of the Lord." It is a warning to those who have lost their appetite for the Word of the Lord. So be careful because one thing God hates is indifference! Apathy towards the Bible will disqualify you from this journey and the ability to receive your inheritance as a child of God. "Please Papa, protect me and my garden from this famine!!!"

I say goodbye to 2016 and watch with eager anticipation what the Lord will bring in 2017; the journey's final year!

FINAL DESCENT
Year Seven

It is 2017, the year of jubilee: which means freedom!

So here we go on the final descent to the center of the garden and this year starts out with a bang! It is Superbowl weekend and I decide to spend most of it relaxing and working on this book. I could sense the Lord beginning to stir up some restlessness in my spirit. It comes from a great deal of anticipation as to what this final descent would require of me and what it could possibly lead to. I have been on this journey my whole life but have been putting it into words from my blood, sweat and tears for the past six years. It's like watching a movie for the past two hours and knowing that the ending is fifteen minutes away; you just gotta hang in there!

So after about a forty-eight hour stretch of writing, reading and re-writing I took a pause to watch some television. I come across one of the Christian channels and see a pastor I know talking about his book, 'The Comeback' and how he made his comeback from the brink of what he thought was death. It turns out it was really his comeback from a real phobia he was suffering called the 'Fear of Death'. The true name of this phobia is 'Thanatophobia', an abnormal, intense or irrational fear of death. When this Phobia grips you it can lead to a great deal of anxiety and a myriad of physical ailments as well. I know the reality of this abnormal fear in me because of my writing last year about the Pop Warner football physical I took when I was eight years old. Being called out for high blood pressure and left alone to my thoughts of an early death is when I believe this fear from the enemy gripped my heart. I know I have claustrophobia, because I am terrified of tight spaces and even being underwater. I think these somehow come with the fear of death. Freud also said that people who express death related fears actually are trying to deal with unresolved childhood conflicts that they cannot come to terms with or express emotions towards. Wow! The re-parenting of God in my life is starting to make more and more sense. I am also beginning to sense that this 'Final Descent' is going to have something to do with the conquering of this fear!

Now after hearing the story of the 'Comeback' and being exposed to this fear of death phobia, I start to drift off on the couch in a cloud of despair. I begin to dream about the day I would be free from this fear that has gripped my heart since childhood. I wonder if I could ever achieve that 'Peace' Jesus said that He came to this earth to give me. How would I make that peace a reality in my life? So I just close my eyes and I begin to pray, "Papa, Please help me to eradicate this fear from my heart! I want to know that peace that Jesus promised and to walk in freedom no matter what the circumstances are in my life! Please Papa, I am so tired from carrying this fear all my life and I don't know if I'll have the strength to finish the journey!" It wasn't a pity party; it was absolutely a cry for help! I rested throughout the night watching some movies while mixing in the Superbowl, then to finally fall into a deep sleep. I awoke the next morning with a loaded schedule that included a trip into Atlanta and as I leave my house I realize I am low on fuel. So before I get to my office and load my car for a busy day, I stop at a gas station to fuel up. After I swipe my credit card and begin pumping gas into my car, the screen on the pump begins to play messages and advertisements. The very first thing that pops up on the screen was from Dictionary.com and it was going to share with me the word of the day and it was a doozy! The word of the day February 6th 2017, was, 'ATARAXIA' definition; a state of freedom from emotional disturbance and anxiety; tranquility.' Come 'on man!!! Are you kidding me!!! Who could do that but God!!! Don't even think for a second that was a coincidence! I spent the last eighteen hours dreaming of the freedom from the fear of death with all its anxieties, heaviness, other phobias and all its physical ailments, only to wonder what it would be like to be free of it all. I don't have to wonder anymore because it is called "Ataraxia'! I just have to get there! Where could 'Ataraxia' be? Is that where the final descent leads to? Only way to find out is to keep on moving down the road. But I have this huge sense that it is going to require crossing another bridge at some point!

WAITING ON GOD

It took me an entire day to actually let what just happened at the gas pump sink into my soul. I had to just sit and let the sequence of events the previous day ruminate in my mind. Questions like, "How did you line everything up so perfectly Papa?" "How did you piece it all together at just the perfect times for it to play out like it did?" "The timing of it all just blew my mind, how did you do it?" these and many more questions flowed through mind all day long. The timing of this answered prayer was so perfect it just left me in awe! And that's when I started to realize what was beginning to come to light in my soul; a truth was being planted in me. This truth would help me understand so much more about this entire journey and its purpose. That truth is," **God's miracles are best experienced in His perfect timing!**" Wow! That's what God is teaching me. His miracles can be seen best if you look to their timing. It's the timing of the miracle that makes it so powerful. And the only way you can you can learn and experience this truth is by waiting on God!

Waiting on God might be the most important underlying principal of God that is required to complete this journey. This principle was at its peak in my journey a few years back when I talked about the chrysalis stage I went through in order to become the person God wanted me to be; It paralleled to the crossing of the bridge from 'Behavior Modification' to 'Character Transformation'. During my chrysalis experience I had to simply wait on God to do what only He could do in me in order for me to be transformed in my character to the likeness of Christ. Waiting on God deals with so many of the ill effects we have ingested from the wasteland period of our life. During the waiting periods of this journey God's transforming power works in us and leads to supernatural transformation that is best shown to us in Isaiah chapter (40: 30-31), "Though youths grow weary and tired and vigorous young men stumble badly, Yet those who wait upon the Lord will gain new strength;" Waiting allows us to exchange our weak and exhaustible source of strength known as the flesh which causes us to 'stumble' through life for God's supernatural power which is absolutely necessary to finish this journey!

Waiting has many more purposes than just receiving the supernatural strength of God. It helps us develop the perseverance needed to make it through the trials necessary to shape our character. Which we now know leads to us developing into mature and complete children of God. It also develops stability in us which we saw last year in the healing of our emotions or the development of our emotional IQ. Maybe more importantly of all it gives us peace. It helps eradicate the anxiety leftover from the wasteland in our souls. Sitting and waiting for God, especially in silence is required to get were God wants to take us.

Waiting on God in silence has become the cornerstone of my quiet time. Over the past several years I have noticed my desire to talk and pray in my own words during my early morning quiet time diminish severely. It has come to the point where I read God's word and then just sit there and listen to Him speak to me as His thoughts ruminate in my mind! I have come to the conclusion, why sit there and tell God what I think I myself or others need and to presume to know what is best for us, and then ask for it. Why not just sit and listen to the one who already knows what I need and has already met that need. Who am I to instruct God?! Ecclesiastes 6:11 says it best, "The more the words, the less the meaning, and how does that profit anyone?" This is also why again, the very first lesson we are taught upon entering the garden is to learn to hear the voice of God. Sitting in silence allows us to develop ears that can hear GOD. We are not born with them; our natural ears are deaf to the voice of God. We must train ourselves to hear His voice and that requires waiting in silence.

What I have also discovered in this time of waiting is that there are certain truths about God that can only be learned in waiting upon Him. We can only receive certain promises of God in the processing of waiting on Him because many promises require that perfect timing to come to fruition. And if we run out ahead of him in impatience we will only make things worse and sabotage His best for us. Look to Abraham and Sarah! God's promises are like seeds for our gardens, they require a gestation period once planted in our hearts. Waiting on God is that gestation period!

Let me also share with you the hardest part of waiting on God; waiting when there seems to be nothing going on! When our lives are full of activity and we are in what seems to be constant motion, waiting can then be somewhat tolerated. But what about the times of waiting when there appears to be zero activity in our lives; No one to date, no activities on the calendar, no job prospect, no appointments scheduled and no one is picking up their phone to answer your call! What then? Would you still wait? Would the stillness and aloneness get you to take matters into your own hands? Would you think God has forgotten you? Or would you be willing to believe that He has your back and is working on your behalf? Because if you're his child; He does have your back and is working diligently for your good. We never make our situation better by thinking we can help God with our situation. We only make things worse!

Therefore, for the sake of our journey to the garden let's heed the words of the Psalmist (Chapter 62), "My soul waits in silence for God only, from Him is my salvation… My soul, wait in silence for God only, for my hope is from Him." God is worth waiting for; He is the only one worth waiting on! To have made it this far in the journey from the wasteland to nearing the garden, waiting on God in silence and alone was a non-negotiable!

THE CROSS IN ME

As I sat alone in silence with God earlier this year He began to unveil one of those truths one gets to learn while waiting on Him and sitting in silence. If you attend church regularly you will often hear about the many benefits that the Cross has done for us as believers. But what I heard God say to me this year on my final descent to the garden was He wanted me to understand what the Cross has done in me. I needed to understand what it was that I was delivered from at the Cross in order to enter the center of the garden. And what I heard Him say to me was, "The Cross has delivered you from 'this present evil age!' Did you know we live in a present evil age? The 2000 years since the Cross is known as an 'evil age.' This age is one giant wasteland of evil, self-centeredness, lies and a prison of fear. Our promise of this deliverance is found in Galatians 1:3, "Grace and peace to you from God our Father and the Lord Jesus Christ, who gave himself for our sins to rescue us from this present evil age…"

So as I sat there contemplating what I just heard I remember early on in my journey that God told me He was on a rescue mission and Jesus was my rescuer. Everything is becoming clearer as I near the garden. Our Enemy, the Devil, wants to hide this truth from the entire world. He has succeeded with non-believers, but has also had great success with believers as well. There are many believers in Christ who still remain in the wasteland and are captivated or ensnared by the deception of the Enemy even though in reality they have already been rescued. That's why Jesus said 27 times in the New Testament, His number one command, "Do not be deceived!" Captivity in the wasteland is a choice. Some choose to stay in the wasteland simply because they enjoy the things of the world or this evil age. Look at Demas, Paul's trusted co-worker, he left Paul's side as stated in 2nd Timothy 4-10,"for Demas, because he loved this world (present evil age), has deserted me..." Again, the Enemy wants to hide the truth about our deliverance from this present evil age from us so he can keep us in the wasteland. Please don't buy the lie! It took me 15 years to muster up the courage to walk out of the false prison known as the wasteland. My get out of jail free card was brokenness! Brokenness is what gave me the courage to walk out of the prison in the wasteland. Again, brokenness is a gift from God!

So what happens when you are exposed to the truth about the 'Cross in me (you)? I believe we cross another bridge, the one from 'Darkness' to 'Light'. As I have journeyed the past 7 years from the wasteland to the garden one thing I have definitely noticed was the darkness and coolness of the wasteland begin to turn into the brightness and warmth of the garden. It happened gradually over time as I walked out this journey. Even now, as I get closer to the actual garden I can begin to see the lights up ahead getting brighter. There is also a distinct aroma I am beginning to get a whiff of and it is heavenly. Not to mention I also am beginning to hear what sounds like a song or an anthem being sung in the center of the garden as well! It is getting close; better keep the sun glasses on!

THE GATE

Back in May of this year a dear friend of mine told me that the Lord revealed to her that I should begin immediately to read Proverbs 31 every day and do it indefinitely. This is someone I know cares deeply for me and intercedes for me in prayer often. I took her at her word and began to do so the very next morning in my quiet time. After about a week or two I began to notice certain things about the chapter that I have not heard about whenever someone would talk about Proverbs 31. You will almost always here people talk of proverbs 31 women, or a 'P-31 woman'. But you never hear about the man in the chapter. But I believe that is what God wanted me to focus on, her husband, the proverbs 31 man, or the 'P-31 man!'

Now, Proverbs 31:10 starts out by saying, "A wife of noble character who can find?" That's a powerful statement. It tells me two things: She is not someone you can just find out in the dating world, she is elusive and must be brought to the one God has chosen for her. Also, if there is anyone who could possibly find her on his own, it would be the P-31 man, but chances are still better that God will lead him to her.

So what is so special about this P-31 man? It is that he is 'respected at the city gate!" (Verse 23) It's where he, "takes his seat among the elders of the land." This is no ordinary Joe and he's definitely not a Schleprock! He is a man purposed and shaped by God to be a pillar in his community. In the Bible the city gate is the main meeting place of the city or community where all the important dealings take place. It is where the prominent members of the community come together to discuss and conduct every aspect of life and business. It's where the big boys play!

It is also where the P-31 woman receives her praise for the woman she is, "Give her the reward she has earned, and let her works bring her praise at the city gate." (Chapter 31, Verse 31) Could it be in the city gate where these two meet? Absolutely! These two have taken the advice to become the person that the person they are looking for, is looking for! They both desire a Godly mate but have decided not to pursue one, but yet more importantly become one! Therefore positioning them for a life together in the center of the garden!

Let me be honest with you, I have spent the past 23 years of my life seeking to become the kind of man that is respected at the city gate. This 7 year journey of brokenness has been just one part of my entire journey. It has been the most difficult but yet at the same times most rewarding. God has been extremely gentle and purposeful with me to bring me out of the wasteland and to arrive at this point of the journey, the city gate. As I stand here I am at awe with God and what He has done in me. The development of my character was brutal and painful at times, the waiting was unbearable at certain points, but God never abandoned me and therefore instilled in me the perseverance to make it here to the city gate. I feel confident that I belong, but also realize there is a long way still to go.

The word Eden means gateway! Could this city gate be the gateway to the garden (EDEN)? I believe it is! I have walked for 83 months of this 84 month journey to get here and it feels amazing! Just standing here looking up and around at this enormous structure that looks like it took a thousand years to build has me flabbergasted! My heart pounds with anticipation that I am ever so close to passing through this gate to what lies on the other side. I'm just going to sit and take my place for a moment and absorb it all in as my soul prepares to walk through. "Thank you Papa for bringing me to this point!"

But as I sit here, I want to speak to you who have followed me on this journey and have kept reading up until this point. If for whatever reason you feel as if you are still in the wasteland of life and have not begun your journey home to the garden, let me send out to you a call to action because that is what this book is about. God never intended for anyone to live in the wasteland. He wants to rescue every person ever to be born and who is attempting to live this thing called life, from the wasteland. This call to action comes to me as I sit here at the city gate waiting to enter the garden. I am reminded of the four lepers in 2nd Kings. They too were in a search for life as they sat at the city gate and pondered what to do in order to survive the famine they were in. They were desperate just as every soul in the wasteland is desperate. So they posed to themselves the question I would pose to everyone reading this that is desperate: Chapter 7: verse 3 says, "Now there were four men with leprosy at the entrance of the city gate (notice where they are as they contemplate life!). They said to each other, "Why sit here until we die?" That is the exact question God is posing to you at this very moment! Why sit here in the wasteland waiting to die? Why not take the journey to the Garden and live? What are you going to do?

RHYTHM OF GOD

As I sit here in the city gate waiting on God and preparing my soul to enter the garden a theme begins to develop. It is as if everything inside me and everyone around me is starting to line up. It is as if a new rhythm is flowing in and through me. I can sense it because it seems to balance everything out and flows with such ease. Then I break into this conversation with God as He begins to instruct me about what is happening. "Listen my son; I am fine tuning your rhythm to flow with mine because it's how we move in the garden!" This is another powerful truth that is implanted in us by waiting on God. In the quietness of waiting, God can fine tune our spirit to His. I believe this whole universe of God's creation is like a symphony and his children are instruments among it. But because of the fall in the original Garden of Eden, we have become out of tune with the Spirit of God. Our Godly rhythm must be restored.

God first exposed this truth to me back in April 2012 while I was visiting my sister in hospice. She was hanging on to life although physically she had nothing left. The doctors suggested that she may want to see certain people before she would let go of this world. So I decided to go there and visit with her and see if I could help facilitate the process of her letting go. As I arrived at hospice I found my family members exhausted and in need of a break so I volunteered to sit with her by myself as they all went home for a five hour break. I sat next to her bed holding her hand believing she could hear me and continually prayed Psalm 23 over her, telling her it was okay to go and that both our earthly Father and heavenly father would welcome her home. It was while I was sitting there that I heard the Holy Spirit whisper to me, "I want to teach you something!" I then felt lead to take the recliner I was sitting in and move it next to her bed, but facing the opposite direction she was. We were now looking at each other face to face. I then reclined my chair all the way down, grabbed her hand and said to her, "Let's take a nap sweetheart!" So we both lay there holding hands and begin to breathe together as I begin to drift off. But then it hit me, our breathing was in sync; it had a beautiful perfect rhythm. I would breathe in while she breathed out and vice versa. We were flowing in our breathing as if we were one person. It was like we were rocking each other to sleep, it was so relaxed and peaceful. I then remember hearing this voice tell me, "That's how I want you and me to be!" I knew it was God!

God wants us in rhythm with Him and not the world. To enter the garden is to set us free from the Enemy's frequency; the frequency of the world and all of its selfishness and lies! To stay in this rhythm is to stay in a position of waiting on God. Those who wait upon the Lord shall be blessed with the rhythm of God. I believe by entering into the garden we are set free from the Enemy's rhythm which is completely out of tune with God!

The rhythm God showed me back in 2012 is now fully in motion and it begins to gently lead me towards the door at the entrance to the garden. I am about to explode!

THE DAY THE DOOR OPENED

It is 12:49 a.m., early in the morning of Tuesday, November 28th 2017. I am lying in bed sound asleep and for the second time in my journey I hear God whisper in my ear "Psssss!" I awake and look around the room to see no one, and immediately know its God! Reluctantly I roll over and say to Him, "What Papa?" He says back to me, "Get up! I'm taking you into the Garden right now! Hurry, the doors about to open!" I'm thinking to myself "Are you serious?" I've been walking and waiting for 83 months with one month to go and I finally get the call! Could it be true? Am I really about to go in? Can I handle this? Will it be what I expected? Could I possibly be let down? Is it a real place? These and many more thoughts raced through my mind as I lay there staring upward. Then I began to realize that it has to be true because that's how God operates; expect it when you least expect it! I mean it's the middle of the night with no warning or inclination that this was the time; just kind of snuck up on me like a thief in the night! But with the little breathe I had left from my state of euphoria I said, "I'm ready!"

As the door slowly opens I instantly sense three things, the aroma, the sound and the light; it was unimaginable. The smell reminded me of the soap house at the farm in South Carolina where I go to make soap. Every heavenly scent you can imagine going in and out of your nostrils at the same time, yet equaling one perfect scent! The sound of a universe in perfect harmony is resonating in my ears, with every part of creation from the plants, to the animals, to the stars and the moon participating in this heavenly choir! And the light, so gentle! Except there is no light, its God's presence that lights the Garden! I walk in and take my first step and my bare feet land on the softest, greenest grass one could ever experience. But probably more amazing than the smell, sound and light, was the sense that fear wasn't there! It wasn't allowed in. It had no place in the garden. Try to imagine that for a moment or two. No fear! If you live on this earth and have never entered the garden you can't comprehend the notion of 'no fear'.

The Enemy rules the earth with fear; it's his M.O. At this moment I'm not only imagining it but about to experience the garden as well.

As I stand there in awe, just a step or two into the garden, I realize what I am about to taste and see is going to be amazing! So with God gently holding my hand we start walking and I know without hesitation I'm not to utter a word: just soak it all up as God unfolds its mystery!

THE BRIDGE FROM 'THANATOPHOBIA' TO 'ATARAXIA'

About a week after my gas station encounter with the word 'Ataraxtia' (s state of freedom from emotional disturbance and anxiety) earlier in February this year I was literally knocked out of my chair while reading the book of Hebrews during one of my morning quiet times. My plan that morning was to read the first three chapters of Hebrews. But when I got to the second chapter I was stopped in my tracks. Now I have read the book of Hebrews no less than twenty-five times in my Christian life. I have read the verses I'm about to share every time I read the book of Hebrews. But it is as if the Holy Spirit had shielded my eyes from them up until now so He could bring them to life at this very moment. These are the verses I came across that morning that will change my life forever and bring the garden to life for me (Hebrews 2:14-15), "Since the children have flesh and blood, he (Jesus) too shared in their humanity so that by his death he might destroy him who holds the power of death – that is, the devil – and free those who all their lives were held in slavery by their fear of death." BOOM!!! There it is! JUBILEE!!! Freedom from the fear of death! The very first thing God wanted to pronounce jubilee upon in my life this year was the fear of death. He saved these two verses for the perfect time in my life, the entering of the garden. By waiting on God, He was now able to set me free from the 'MOAF': the mother of all fears! The crossing from 'Tanatophobia' to 'Ataraxia' is the main purpose of the garden. Removing the fear of death sets one free to receive the peace that Jesus promises to his children (John 14:27), "Peace I leave with you; my peace I give you. I do not give to you as the world gives. Do not let your hearts be troubled and do not be afraid."

The bridge from 'Tanatophobia' to 'Ataraxia' was crossed at the cross. Jesus already made the exchange. We just have to receive it and that's what we do when we enter garden. Entering the garden, leaving 'Tanatophobia' and receiving 'Ataraxia' is getting set free from Satan's frequency and getting into the rhythm of God. So now let me paint you a picture of what I experienced as I crossed this bridge to the center of the garden. It is the experience I hope every child of God will be able to receive while on this earth in this fallen, broken world.

THE CENTER OF THE GARDEN

As God and I start walking across the bridge from 'Tanatophobia' to 'Ataraxia', my eyes became so wide open and my vision was crystal clear. The sights and sounds, as well as the aroma were utterly amazing! Walking was fluent because everything was in perfect rhythm. I was barefoot and the grass beneath my feet was so soft it was as if I was receiving a foot massage with every step. But what I saw in front of me sent exhilaration through my entire being. I saw a vast ocean of crystal clear blue water filled with every sea creature there was and they were singing the song of the universe and it was rising off the ocean's floor. The ocean's surface was smooth as glass and reflected God's glory, even as the sea creatures swam through it. The sky above the ocean was so soft and filled with more stars than any human being could count. This ocean was so vast it seemed to have no boundaries and went on forever. Crossing this ocean seemed to me an impossible task.

But as I stood there in wonder and amazement, it happened; the ocean began to part! It was as if God's finger started moving across the surface creating a wake which eventually grew to the point of complete separation of the water. God had split the ocean in two, and what moments ago seemed impossible to cross was now dry land leading to the other side. I wanted to run as fast as I could to see what awaited us, but knew best to not run out ahead of God and miss the miracle I knew I was about to witness. It needed to be shown to me in His perfect time. So I walked with God in shear amazement that I too was experiencing what His natural children, the Israelites experienced about thirty-five hundred years ago. To walk this walk was phenomenal. It felt like I was leaving fear behind and that the way out of bondage to fear was through a parted sea. It's again a beautiful picture of how God leads His children out of bondage! If the Israelites felt anything like I do at the moment they would have been filled with excitement, anxiety and vulnerability all at the same time as they traversed the dry floor of the sea! Crossing the parted sea is the passage every child of God must take if their true heart's desire is to be released from bondage!

As God and I walked together hand in hand through the two giant walls of sea that looked like an aquarium straight out of heaven itself, I could not help but feel completely loved and accepted by him; I felt as if I truly belonged to him, I was all His! I had lost that feeling, that lie that told me I have been alone since I was three years old! But I was in such awe of what was happening I couldn't speak, I couldn't utter a word. I just had to let the love I was feeling begin to permeate my spirit, soul and body! It was as if I could actually begin to feel the perfect love of God filling up my soul and driving the fear right out of me! I wasn't about to do anything but stay in the moment!

We walked like a daddy holding his little boy's hand for a while through the sea when all of a sudden the aroma, the sound and the light all began to heighten and I could see we were coming to the end of the road. The seven year journey was about to reach its climax. Every step I took from this moment on was pure grace. These steps were given to those who said 'yes' to this journey and did not shrink back when things got tough. They were given to those who understood that the reward of saying 'yes' was greater than the regret of saying 'no' to God's invitation to journey out of the wasteland to the center of the garden. Every step I took over the past seven years was writing myself into the story of God; His story was becoming my story. I realize now it is better for our little story to be part of God's big story than it is to try and make our story bigger! In other words, "don't go it alone!" Two are better than one! God is worth the risk! He is worth saying 'yes' to the journey of brokenness! And for those who say 'yes' here's what happens next!

Every single day for seven years, ever since I said 'yes' to God's invitation to take this journey, I have wondered and tried to imagine what would await me at the climactic end of it all. It is said best in 1st Corinthians 2:9, "What no eye has seen, what no ear has heard, what no human mind has conceived - the things God has prepared for those who love him." So I try now to clear my thoughts, empty my mind and just receive what I'm about to experience: the center of the garden! Here we go!

God and I come to the end of the road and the sea closes behind us. I see and archway gate and the two of us walk through and its show time! I see a massive city lit up like Times Square at Christmas times a billion. The streets are paved in gold and lined with fruit trees bearing fruits of all kinds at the same time. A river runs through it that is filled with crystal clear water and has an amazing fragrance of tears. The city is lit with the love of God, no need for electricity. There is no chaos in this city. Everything flows in perfect harmony with the rhythm of God. The people are at rest: no worries, no anxiety, and no fear! Faith guides every one of their steps: no wrong turns, no side tracks and no Banging-Ueys! But the greatest thing of all is what took place next!

Just when I think it couldn't possibly get any better, I hear my name being called from the city's center court! God then let's go of my hand and says to me "go ahead this is for you!" With a smile as wide as the Grand Canyon I take off running toward the center court. As I get close I see that it is filled with all the garden dwelling saints and they begin to separate as to clear a path for me straight to the middle of the crowd: It kind of felt like I was running down a tunnel into a packed stadium ready to play in the super bowl with the crowd going crazy. But this was better! It wasn't the super bowl which lasts for only a few hours, this felt as if it would last forever. And the people weren't going crazy, they were singing! So with the greatest anticipation I have ever felt I run through the crowd and come into the center court where I take my stand on what looked to be a mini mountain top and I just stood there before the crowd knowing it was my time and this was my welcome home party! And as I stood there with my feet firmly planted and my arms wide open I began to sing the Anthem of the center of the garden "I'm no longer a slave to fear; I am a child of God!" I sang along with all the other saints. I had earned the privilege to sing what would now become my Anthem as well!

All of my life I have dreamed and wondered what it would truly be like if I knew that I was accepted and loved unconditionally; that I truly belonged to a family. As I stood there on that mini mountain top in the center court of the center of the garden surrounded by my brothers and sisters with my arms flung wide open singing and shouting "I am a child of

God", my dream came true! I knew at that moment life would never be the same! I am His! No separation! God called me to this from my mother's womb where he knit me together and purposed me as one of his own. I am now rescued and am no longer one of those who for their whole life have been held in slavery to the fear of death. I am liberated from my bondage! I have arrived at Ataraxia!

We were never meant to live in the wasteland. God's original plan was for us was to live here in the garden and have perfect communion with Him. Our original ears would've been able to hear the voice of God like Adam and Eve did in the beginning before the fall. But sin entered the world and we all went deaf to God. We now need a great deal of training to hear the voice of God so that he may walk us out of the wasteland and into the garden. Trust me. You want to be here! If you listen to anything I've written in this book listen to this, "You want to be here! You want to live in the center of garden! You will regret saying no to this journey now and especially in eternity. The reward of saying yes to this journey is unfathomable to those in the wasteland, but is absolutely, undeniably worth the risk to say yes to God's invitation to the journey!

"Yet to all who did receive him, to those who believed in his name, he gave the right to become children of God—" (John 1:12)

GLIMPSES OF ETERNITY

Why would you want to be here in the center of the garden you may ask? In the book of Ecclesiastes 3:11 says, "He has made everything beautiful in its time. He has also set eternity in the hearts of men; yet they cannot fathom what God has done from beginning to end." We live in this broken, fallen world tainted by sin, separated from God. It's not an easy place to live. But to those called, chosen and who receive Him (Jesus), there is a solution. It's the garden, Ataraxia; A place deep in your soul free from the slavery to the fear of death and all its tentacles. A place where we can experience what I call glimpses of eternity. Though we may live in the broken world of fear, we can still find a taste of heaven in our souls when needed; times of refreshing! That is the purpose of God leading us out of this wasteland called the world and delivering us from this present evil age of darkness and fear. He is prepping us for eternity with him! And by giving us these glimpses of eternity in the center of the garden while still living on this planet our hearts begin to line up with his and we begin to get a taste of what's to come when we actually enter into eternity with him.

What is a 'glimpse of eternity'? I believe this book is full of them. Every time I mention hearing the voice of God in my spirit, it is a glimpse of eternity; The "PSSSSS" in the middle of the night or in the middle of verbal tirade from your enemy that says to you, "I got this!" That voice behind you as you walk this journey saying to you, "go this way, go that way!" Finding yourself in the right place, at the right time, with the right person over and over again! The last second bailouts that you didn't see coming and had no idea where they could possibly come from! The phone call you needed at just the perfect time to ease your heavy burden. And there are the mindblowers like this year when I arrived at the gas station to see my prayer answered on the video screen of a gas pump!!! What I want you to know most about these glimpses of eternity is that they happen exponentially more when you are in the center of the garden than anywhere else. They can actually become a daily occurrence. They start to become the norm and life begins to flourish like a well-watered garden from these glimpses of eternity. You will start to believe that God is for you all the time, even during the severe trials of life. Like James said, you will begin to count it all joy when you face trials and tribulations of various kinds while living in the center of the garden. Don't you want to live that way?!!! Are you not tired of the strife of life? Do you not want to see the Mocker in you be driven out of you so that the Lover in you can flourish?! Do you not want to be someone who continually fills others up instead being a constant drain on them? Don't you want to dream big with God? To throw off everything that so easily entangles you in order to pursue those dreams? Don't you want to live the unexplainable life? When half your conversations in life start with, "You're not going to believe what God did this time?!!!

If you are like me and your heart desires nothing more, nothing less than God's best, say 'YES' to the invite to take the journey from the wasteland to the garden. I'll tell you why next!

IT'S A REAL PLACE

If there is anything I can assure you of in this life, it is that you want to say 'Yes' to your invitation to leave the wasteland and enter the garden. You may be thinking that everything I told you sounds great if it were true. That it would be nice to be there if it really existed. Let me drop a truth bomb on you, "It's a real place!" And for those who have made it deep down in their soul to the center of the garden, who know beyond a doubt that they are a child of God and no longer a slave to fear, they know the reality of this place. They endured the journey of brokenness and life is very different; it is truly a life at rest while seemingly going a million miles an hour. They didn't fall for the self-help trap, they said goodbye to self!!! They understand that the way up in the garden of God's kingdom is down. They don't prop up their lives they lay them down. You too can live in this reality. You need to believe that it is real and attainable in order to start. Otherwise the enemy will be able to convince you that the journey isn't worth the risk because the destination might not exist. It absolutely does and it is Ataraxia! You have crossed the Galatians 2:20 bridge and Jesus Christ has now become your life! Knowing you are perfect and complete in Christ changes everything. The pain of the wasteland disappears.

TIME TO LET GO

What are you holding onto? That's an important question in life because it has huge consequences. I learned of these consequences in January of 2005. I was visiting a client down in Florida and he had a friend who was generous to let me stay at his guest house which just happened to have about five little ponds on the property that were all good for some bass fishing. On the morning of my last day there I decided to take advantage of the ponds and awoke early to go out and do some fishing. About an hour or so into fishing the gentlemen who owned the property came driving in. He was an elderly man, but also a very godly man as I soon came to find out.

Now it turns out I am fishing in a specific corner of one of the ponds that is a very emotional place for him. This was no coincidence; the Lord had set this one up perfectly (Glimpse of Eternity)! He pulls up his truck gets out and we begin a conversation in which he starts to unload some nuggets of wisdom into my soul. He told me that he discovered that listening to the voice of God was our number one priority in life and that we were to shut down our listening to all the other voices that were trying to get our ear; sound familiar? He then says to me, "Let me tell you a story about this very spot you are fishing in!" A story that would rock my world!

He then begins telling me that about forty years ago his two elderly parents decided to get in a little boat on cold January afternoon in this very pond to just enjoy the day but something had caused the boat to tip over and sent the two of them into a panic in freezing water. Now right at the spot where this took place lay a fallen tree that was protruding somewhat out of the water and the two of them managed to grab onto the tree and hold on for dear life! This gentleman was the first to arrive at the scene and immediately called 911. Unfortunately as they went into the pond to rescue the parents his mom was already deceased and his father soon passed away on the way to the hospitable, both from hypothermia. This gentleman then proceeds to tell me that he walked around the pond every day for six months listening to God and waiting for an answer to what had happened.

Then it strikes him, the 'AHA' moment! He remembers the day that they cut the tree down that lay in the water; it was before the pond was filled. He realizes that the water depth were the parents were found holding onto the tree was only about four to five feet deep. If they had only let go of the tree they could of set their feet on the ground and walked out of the pond to live another day! Wow!!! Then he lays on me the wisdom that changed me forever. He looks at me and says, "If you hold onto something long enough it will kill you! What are you holding onto son?"

That rocked me to my soul's core. I went to bed that night and just like Jacob I wrestled with an angel of God for several hours. I held onto that angel's leg and wasn't going to let go. It was so intense that I finally had to get out of bed at about 2:30 a.m., pack my bag and take off on a six hour drive home. Little did I know that was a huge step in Papa's leading me to my brokenness in 2010? I now realize I was holding onto my life and I needed to let it go. It had to fall to the ground and die if it were to become more seed and produce more crops!

What are you holding onto to? Do you think it is time to let go of whatever? You can't take this journey while still holding onto your old life, you have to let go! How bad do you want to leave the wasteland and go live in the center of the garden? How bad to you want to go to your welcome home party in the center court? How bad to you want God's best for your life? Hey, from someone writing to you from the center court of the center of the garden, listen to me: You should want it more than your own life! You only have one lifetime, one shot at making it to the center of the garden here on earth. Why would you not let go of it all and go for God's best? Here's why: FEAR! And that's the purpose of this journey; freedom from fear! There is no greater life; this is really no other life at all!

THE SUM OF IT ALL

This seven year journey can be summarized in the 17th chapter of the book of Jeremiah. God showed me these verses at the very beginning of my journey and told me to hold onto them till now. Brokenness is the bridge on the journey from 'Jeremiah 17:5-6' to 'Jeremiah 17:7-8'! Finishing your journey from the wasteland to the garden will take you out of Jeremiah 17:5-6 and land you smack dab in the center of Jeremiah 17:7-8. Our life before brokenness, the wasteland, is described as so, Jeremiah 17:5-6, "Cursed is the one who trust in man, who depends on flesh for his strength and who's heart turns away from the Lord. He will be like a bush in the wastelands; he will not see prosperity when it comes. He will dwell in the parched places of the desert, in a salt land where no one lives." Are you kidding me?!!! Does this not describe in complete detail the life of one who lives in the wasteland? Are you sure you want to stay there till you die? It's time to stop trusting in the flesh, our own efforts! Hearts need to be turned back to God in these final days. Prosperity, real kingdom prosperity, not so much the earthly kind, is awaiting you in the garden. Listen to Jeremiah, "no one lives" in the wasteland. You only sit there and survive till you die. Please don't do that to yourself! Say 'YES' to the invitation to leave the wasteland. Say 'YES' to brokenness, the bridge that takes you to the garden. Yes, it is tough, brutal, painful and unbearable at times, but look where it takes you; Jeremiah 17:7-8, "But blessed is the man who trusts in the Lord, whose confidence is in him. He will be like a tree planted by the water that sends out it roots by the stream. It does not fear when heat comes; its leaves are always green. It has no worries in a year of drought and never fails to bear fruit." Are you kidding me again?!!!! Doesn't that describe the garden?! That's what I'm talking about; garden living! It is entirely a new way of life; Matter of fact that is life, not survival and death like the wasteland. Come on man! How bad do you want it?!!!!!!!

If you do want it, life in the garden, you have a promise from God and it is found in the book of Isaiah 51:3, "The Lord will surely comfort Zion and will look with compassion on all her ruins; he will make her deserts like Eden, her wastelands like the garden of the Lord." The one thing God can't do is lie! But this promise only goes to the one who says 'YES' to the invitation of brokenness, the one who is willing to risk it all for the sake of the Kingdom and enter the arena where the battles are fierce, the enemy is corrupt and rules don't apply; but where God has your back.

THE BEGINNING, NOT THE END

The final descent to the center of the garden was taken by Jesus at the cross and it is his way of getting to the absolute core of our hearts and the center of our gardens. It is this final descent that allows perfect love to cast out all fear. Jesus made this final descent into the abyss the very second he took His last breath on the cross and conquered the enemy and his scandal of fear once and for all. It is time for this garden life to become real in our hearts. I believe it is time for my garden to be in full bloom and answer the call every saint hears once they make it to the center of the garden.

The call I hear in my heart is to become a bridge guide! To go back to my brothers and sisters who are in the wasteland and help them on their journey home to the center of the garden. That is one of the privileges we inherit as garden dwellers. It is not an order, it is a privilege! One I pray I do not take lightly. In fact my prayer is to be the ultimate bridge guide. That's why I recorded my journey, to encourage others to say 'YES' and take their own journey. I want every person who listens to my story to trade their own personal story in and get in on God's story of brokenness for their lives.

I have wondered for seven years what it would be like when this journey ended and I reached the center of the garden. I have taken every step steeped in anticipation as I followed the Holy Spirits guidance along the way. But very early this year God made it very clear to me, "Reaching the center of the garden is not the end of the journey, it's the beginning!" I can only imagine what lies ahead!

So here I come all you inhabitants of the wasteland. I am saying to you, "Why sit there till you die? Let go of it all and start walking." As a matter of fact all of us here in the center of the garden are calling out to you the words of Ezra 10:4, "Rise up; this matter is in your hands. We will support you, so take courage and do it."

MY FIRST GARDEN ASSIGNMENT

A couple of years ago my mom was diagnosed with Dementia. Recently we have seen a quickening of her mind's senses deteriorate. I am not positive but I do not believe my mom to be a believer in Christ. So as Christmas time 2017 drew near I started to feel a sense of desperation knowing that I would head to Florida and possibly spend the last Christmas with my mom knowing who I was. It was a gut wrenching feeling I could not walk away from and needed to reconcile in my soul. Thank God I was now living in the center of the Garden because I could hear the Holy Spirit begin to whisper in my ear words of encouragement to prepare my heart for my first 'Bridge Guide' assignment in the garden!

I started to think this was going to be my last chance to share the Gospel of salvation with my mom and I needed a plan to seize the moment when I arrived in Florida. After sharing my concern for my mom with a friend of mine a plan started to develop. She asked me what my mom's favorite flowers were and I found out that they were lilies and mums. She decided to research the lily plant and found out that it represented the humility of Christ as it gave that appearance from its somewhat bowing or drooping posture. Then it hit me; when I get to Florida surround her with flowers as if she is in the Garden and let the Holy Spirit begin to allure her to Jesus. And that's exactly what I did when I arrived on the morning of December 23rd. I filled her room with three beautiful bouquets of lilies and mums and then went off to the beach for the rest of the day to let the flowers' aroma and beauty fill the room.

The very next morning, Christmas Eve, I decided to go sit with my mom and have some coffee with her. We sat and watched the news for a few minutes until a Christian program came on next on the very same channel we were watching. The preacher in this program spoke about the idea that once we have persevered through the many trials of life and have reached a certain point of trust in God, He will begin to make things easier for us by working on our behalf instead of our own self-effort; basically garden living. When the program ended I could hear God say, "Go for it! I will help you!

That's exactly what I did! I looked at my mom sitting in her chair next to mine and began to talk to her about Jesus and eternity. My final question to her was, "Mama, would you want to ask Jesus into your heart so that you could be with me and daddy in heaven?" And she said, "Yes, I would like that!" I left my chair, took one step and knelt before her to pray with her. As soon as I did that she put out her hands in a receiving posture facing upward as if she was waiting to be handed something. Again I could hear God say, "She is ready to receive!" I put my hands in hers and we prayed together. In that moment she accepted Jesus into her heart and all the angels in heaven rejoiced! God just did in 24 hours what I had tried to do on my own for 24 years. I had led others to Christ many times while I was in my wasteland existence, but this time it was different. This time I sat and watched as God did it all through me; this time it was effortless and easy!

What happened next added to the beauty of that moment. She wouldn't let go of my hands! She just held onto them and began rubbing the top of my hands with her thumbs. I look up and I kid you not; I watch the Holy Spirit begin to fill her! I could see the Spirit of God rise up from her belly to the top of her head. And as my eyes followed that progression in her, my eyes locked on hers and I saw the most beautiful childlike smile I had ever seen on the face of my mom! Her eyes lit up like the sun and were bluer than the bluest sky on a clear day! I sat there for ten more minutes just soaking it up looking into her eyes and thinking what a good, good Father we have! My eighty-two year old mom with Dementia who can barely distinguish fantasy from reality at this point just got saved! My first garden assignment complete! Success! That's the joy of being a bridge guide! That's Garden living!!!

One down, millions to go! So here I come all you inhabitants of the wasteland. I am saying to you, "Why sit there till you die? Let go of it all and start walking."

Until we meet in the center of the garden one day! God Bless you all!

THE CALL

I awoke one morning in January of 2010 to find myself in the fetal position on the edge of my bed in tears. It was my moment of brokenness. God had finally brought me to the very end of myself; I had no will of my own left. Doing life my way apart from God no longer worked; Life as I knew it for 45 years was about to change completely. I would enter the spiritual ICU unit for the entire year of 2010 receiving spiritual nurturing and restoration through counseling.

As soon as I was able to stand on my own two feet again I felt like God wanted me to go straight to spiritual physical therapy so I enrolled in a yearlong course in 2011 to learn my true identity and begin to live it out. It was an incredible experience that absolutely required brokenness as a prerequisite. The journey I was about to be asked to take with God required my total surrender to His will, His leading and the guidance of the Holy Spirit. There was no need nor room for my personal will on this journey because it would only cause trials and delays; it would turn an 11 day journey into 40 years! My journey that lied ahead would require 7 years.

In order to complete the yearlong course I was required to write a paper 12 pages long describing my personal journey over the past year. I immediately panicked! I had never really written a paper on my own before. Even though I had been journaling for the better part of the previous 15 years, I never really put anything together that would resemble a finished work. As painful as this is to say, in high school and college, I had others either help me or totally write my papers for me. And If I couldn't go that route I would buy a paper on the 'black market' already written for that course and have it re-typed to make it look like my own.

But this time there would be no faking it. I had to live and write out of my own identity, my new identity in Christ. So I began the process of sitting down and actually writing my thoughts down on paper. It was excruciating! It took me over 100 hours and 77 rewrites to finish my paper. It was choppy at best, but it was mine. I also felt like it had some depth to it. That it might actually be the start of something pretty cool. The experience of writing it on my own changed something inside of me. It unleashed a desire to continue on my journey and to go places inside me that I had never been willing to go to before. What I heard next from the Lord would blow my mind and leave me with the most anxiety filled sense of excitement that I had ever experienced.

Soon after graduating from the course I was in prayer with God talking about how much I enjoyed writing the paper when I heard Him say to me, "Keep writing!" My response was somewhat hesitant, "what do you mean?" God, "You are going to write a book. It will be a recording of your 7 year journey. You will write a paper a year over the next 6 years, 7 years altogether, and they will culminate into a book in the year after; 2018. But you are never to write on theory, only experience! No one likes a 'know it all', you must walk this journey out and record every experience." So the journey would continue, a 7 year journey; but where does it lead to? Could it be one from the wasteland to the garden? Is there actually a garden, a heavenly one here on earth? Is the journey going to be tough? Fun? Frightening? Exciting? Will I survive at the end? Will I be another Braveheart or Gladiator?

For the next 6 years I walked out my journey with God, the Holy Spirit guiding me every step of the way. I felt every emotion to its extreme. I questioned every lie I was ever told and handed them over to God to be replaced with the truth. I looked at the fear inside me and called it a liar. The journey was brutal at times and I would have despaired and quit had I not chosen to walk through that door of hope. Hope was my anchor so that no matter how hard situations would get I could truly believe that God was in total control and had my back so I could withstand the storm. The best way I can describe the journey was that I felt like Denzel Washington in The Book of Eli. I was told to keep going no matter what. Even when I felt my life was in danger God would always protect me and eventually show me the way out and open a door to the next part of the journey. It was an amazing journey, the ultimate story of redemption and restoration; one I felt I should share with the world.

Now at the end of 2016 as I was finishing the 'Search for Wisdom' the theme to that year's paper, I began to hear the words 'Final Descent' over and over again. It was typical for God to begin to give me the theme to the next paper and the end of every year as I was finishing up the current year's paper. It was in January of 2017 that it was confirmed to me that 'Final Descent' would be the theme for the 7th and final paper. A theme that to me was totally appropriate for the end of the journey. That is because in the first year of the journey I was awakened to the truth that 'the way up in the Kingdom of God is down!' It also became crystal clear that this journey was not one of progress, but of digression, back to the way life was meant to be with God in control and us in paradise; a beautiful garden!

So as I journeyed through 2017 on my 'Final Descent' to what I believed to be a garden, I reached the point in October where I felt led to sit down and begin to write my last paper before turning them all into a book. But something else began to happen that was much unexpected. God began waking me up in the middle of the night for hours at a time and would sit with me and teach me some of the most amazing principles and truths about what was about to happen and where I was about to go. It was if I no longer needed to sleep. I would have endless energy with only an hour or two of sleep. The middle of the night lessons and visions were so amazing that the sheer power of them would energize me for days. I began pinching myself every day to make sure I was still here and hadn't passed on to heaven itself. This went on for six to eight weeks until it climaxed late in November, right in the middle of my writing 'Final Descent'.

It was on November 28th 2017 at 12:49 a.m., that life as I knew it would forever be changed. It was the moment I got the call! I was sound asleep and heard, "PSSSSS! get up, we're about to enter the Garden. Hurry! The door is about to open!" Who could have ever imagined that after 7 years of walking out this journey it would come to a moment like this! Ever since I entered the garden my life has been one amazing moment to the next. Everything has changed, and all for the better. It is the best possible life you can live in this broken and fallen world. It is the glimpse of eternity before we actually get to eternity.

Besides receiving my first assignment of going back to the wasteland and leading my mom to Christ and saving her from the darkness, I was given a second assignment that was specifically for me and was told that it must be met with precision and would be an extremely important exercise in discipline that would benefit me greatly in my calling. It had to do with receiving my inheritance, my elevation to God's best for my life. I was going to receive many upgrades in many areas of life.

You see when you enter the garden everything in your life begins to flourish, so you need a new set of tools to handle it. You need upgrades in your senses to be able to see, hear and speak in your new life in the garden. So you will get a new set of eyes to see as God's sees and a completely new perspective of life. You will get a new set of ears to hear the voice of God instruct you and to hear the Holy spirit guide you. You will also receive a new language and dialogue to communicate with God and be able to share it with the world. You will begin to inherit, or be elevated to God's best in every area of life. The old way of living as the world does, a life lived in the flesh, full of self-will and determination doesn't even appeal to you anymore; your new life of total surrender to God and being at rest, which is Holy Spirit directed activity, flows like a stream of cool water refreshing everything and everyone in its path. Bottom line is that when you enter the garden you begin to receive your God appointed inheritance.

Why is this so important? It is because so many times you read in scripture that so and so will not inherit the kingdom of God (1st Corinthians 6:9-10 and15:50/ Galatians 5:19-21). But what does it mean, "Not to inherit the Kingdom of God?" It means you can't enter the garden here on earth; you won't experience the rest that comes with garden living. You won't receive God's best for your life if that's what you truly desire. You will miss out on your heavenly inheritance here on earth. You will miss out on the glimpses of eternity, that make you smile for days. You simply won't have that peace that surpasses all understanding. You will be trapped in the wasteland trying to manufacture life on your own. Exhausting!!! And trust me when I say these words, "You want to live in the Garden!" You want to be in this place where you have communion with God and an absolute sense that you are in paradise here on earth. Trust me; you want to inherit the Kingdom of God here on earth. That is the goal for everyone who accepts Christ as savior.

MY INHERITANCE

Shortly after leading my mom to Christ and returning home from Florida. I was again wakened in the middle of the night and while listening to God would receive my instructions on the elevation to my inheritance now that I was living in the garden. This would be one of the coolest assignments I would have ever been given in life, actually everything is cooler in the garden, and it's just the way it is in there! I was instructed to read Isaiah 41:8-20 for the next 6 months. I was also instructed not to leave those 12 verses during that time. I was to remain disciplined and read those 12 verses only; for they were my inheritance. I was instructed to take every word in those verses and make them mine. I had to search out each and every word to find the meaning it had for me and my new life. I looked up each word and studied every different way it could be used and every one of its definitions. Then waited for the Holy Spirit to reinterpret that word into my own interpretation and then I would claim it as mine and begin my very own dialogue with God. It was the most amazing transformation of dialogue and scripture that I had ever experienced.

What began to happen next was remarkable. The Bible, specifically these 12 verses started to become part of me. I was inheriting them. When I would read them my spirit would automatically interpret them in the new dialogue I was developing with God. These verses no longer were black words on white paper; they were an intimate dialogue between God and me. Not only that, they were becoming alive and creating the road map to my calling. I began to see the purpose to my entire life up to this point. It was if God took me up to the clouds and gave me a timeline view of my life's journey, and where it was heading. Most of all it had purpose; the desire of every human soul, PURPOSE!!! Why was I born? Didn't seem like such a huge question anymore!

To be honest with you I thought this request from God was a bit elementary. I thought to myself, "I will be done with this assignment in 2-3 weeks! What could I possibly do for the next 5 plus months?" Oh was I ever mistaken. As I wind this assignment down I am a tad bit nervous I won't finish in time. Furthermore, I don't want to finish. I never want to stop inheriting scripture. It is exhilarating to experience and life changing all the way to eternity. Here is Isaiah 41:8-20, followed by my inherited version of those 12 verses which I will refer to as Dario 41: 8-20. Watch what happens to scripture once inherited in the Garden!

ISAIAH; 41: 8-20

8) "But you, O Israel, my servant,
Jacob, whom I have chosen,
you descendants of Abraham my friend.
9) I took you from the ends of the earth,
From its farthest corners I called you.
I said, "You are my servant";
I have chosen you and have not rejected you.
10) So do not fear, for I am with you,
Do not be dismayed, for I am your God.
I will strengthen you and help you;
I will uphold you with my righteous right hand.
11) All who rage against you
Will surely be ashamed and disgraced;
Those who oppose you
Will be as nothing and perish.
12) Though you search for your enemies,
You will not find them.
Those who wage war against you
will be as nothing at all.
13) For I am the Lord, your God,
Who takes hold of your right hand
And says to you, Do not fear;
I will help you.
14) Do not be afraid, O worm Jacob,
O little Israel,
For I myself will help you," declares the Lord,
your Redeemer, the Holy one of Israel.
15) "See, I will make you into a threshing sledge,
new and sharp, with many teeth.
You will thresh the mountains and crush them,
And reduce the hills to chaff.
16) You will winnow them, the wind will pick them up,
and a gale will blow them away.
But you will rejoice in the Lord

And glory in the Holy One of Israel.
17) "The poor and needy search for water,
But there is none;
Their tongues are parched with thirst.
But I the Lord will answer them;
I, the God of Israel, will not forsake them.
18) I will make rivers flow on barren heights,
and springs within the valleys.
I will turn the desert into pools of water,
And the parched ground into springs.
19) I will put in the desert
the cedar and the acacia, the myrtle and the olive.
I will set pines in the wasteland,
the fir and the cypress together,
20) so that people may see and know,
may consider and understand,
that the hand of the Lord has done this,
that the Holy one of Israel has created it.

Here now is my new dialogue with God as interpreted through my new eyes and ears!

Dario; 41: 8-20

8) But you Dario, a descendant of my people,
whom I have dealt with severely,
you belong to me, your Master's slave, a follower
of Christ having full commitment to me
with no will of your own. Brokenness is my gift to
you. You have suffered but will do great
things; your life will be a living example of my restorative work.
You have been selected, hand-picked as the best and most appropriate,
an offspring of Abraham who I know as a
loyal friend with mutual affection.
9) I, the Lord began to like you the most Dario, to
love you and choose you when you were the

farthest away; in your prison of self, a cave, deep
in the far corner of the wasteland.
I traveled that far to retrieve you and rescue
you and I am never going to stop.
I called you to be faithful and trust me, to continue
to actively believe in my goodness.
I say to you Dario,
"You belong to me and no one else, you shall serve no other!
I have full claim of your life;
you shall depend on no other!
And I shall have your full commitment in return."
I have preferred you and favored you above others
and do not consider you inadequate.
I will never turn my back on you;
My affection and concern for you is endless.
10) So do not believe the lies of the enemy or this
world that will cause you to become anxious
and afraid, or you will become apprehensive in
following me. But stand in awe of my greatness
and goodness towards you. I will be accompanying
you because you belong to me.
Do not lose your courage or be disheartened when
sudden danger or trouble appears,
You will deprive yourself of strength and
firmness of mind to stay the course,
For I am your strength and moral authority,
the Holy Spirit your compass.
According to your wishes, I will give you my
strength and make you strong and effective
As well as make it easy for you.
I will support you against all opposition, sustain
and possess you with my divine law,
Moral goodness and power.
11) Everyone, every person and everything that feels
or tries to express uncontrollable anger

And hostility in opposition to you will without
question be regretful and embarrassed
Of their actions as well as lose my respect and fall from my favor.
These specific people I just mentioned who attempt
to prevent your success by actively resisting
You, especially by argument, will have no chance of succeeding.
They will be non-existent after suffering ruin and destruction.
12) Despite the fact that you look high and low to try
and find those people who hate you and are
Actively opposed and hostile toward you Dario,
You will not even notice them and you will pay them no mind.
The aforementioned enemies who carry on a
campaign of conflict and attack you
Will have no value, importance or significance in
your life, you will care nothing for them.
13) I am Jesus, your Master, Ruler; I have all authority
over you and complete control of your
Life and will always act with superiority towards you.
I reach for and support you with my arms and hands
for you are justified and acceptable to me;
This is true as fact.
I utter these words to you for your benefit, do not
express or act upon negative emotions
Based on lies from the enemy.
I will make things easy for you if you put all your confidence in me.
14) Do not be unwilling or reluctant to follow me
because of the fear of consequences,
Or be a weak and despicable person, YOU ARE
MY AFFECTIONATE ONE!
You have no idea how much I will personally help you on this journey,
I give you my unbreakable word; the one who has
brought you back and restored your rights
And revenged your wrongs, the God of the chosen ones.
15) Understand Dario, after reflecting upon
what your eyes have perceived,

I want you to notice that I have put my Spirit
in you, and together with yours,
You will become a machine that separates and tramples out the flesh,
Experienced and keen, possessing numerous means
of effectively using my power of destruction.
You Dario, absolutely will bash, batter and pummel
with repeated strikes the very love of self, as
Well as put to an end those who are vain glorious
and bring those vanities into a less desirable
Place, as your flesh will become worthless.
16) You will separate these vanities of the flesh from my spirit in you,
My force of influence will take hold them and remove them abruptly,
And a strong burst of my power will blast them into non-existence.
Nevertheless Dario, the insecure who lack
confidence, those in need of much attention
And demand a lot of care; those consumed with
self, try blindly to find the source of life,
Though in their current condition no life exists.
Their rebellion and worldly consumption has left
them dry with a strong spiritual desire
For the water of life.
Despite all that, as their Master and Ruler, I will
respond to their cries and am suitable
To fulfill their needs.
I Jehovah Yahweh will not abandon or give up on the destitute.
18) I will cause large natural streams of water
to appear from nowhere to invigorate
You and give you a feeling of energized focus
and clarity into the unproductive,
Unfruitful and lifeless parts of you, this energy
will become a resource within you
To sustain you in the low points of life.
I will change the very nature of this place of abandonment
by filling it with purity and fertility
And those longing for a drink will have their desires fulfilled.

19) I will change the landscape of the desolate
wasteland with conifers that yield
Sweet fragrances, produce durable timber for
construction and are like umbrellas for shade,
And represent My promised blessings in a "good land" full of prosperity,
Beauty and spiritual privilege.
I will turn the wasteland, your spiritually, emotionally
and unsatisfying life into a Garden where
Everything works together for your good.
20) I will do this to such an extent that every
person on this earth will admit that what
They notice about this transformation using their eyes
and have become aware of through careful
Observation, will express hope by thinking
carefully about what they've seen
And become aware of my good intentions.
That by my power, strength and favor I have
completed this transformation,
That I, God, make all things new.

I have now inherited these 12 verses and they have become the foundation to which my calling has been established. I have them in my own personal dialogue with God. I don't have to sit there and read them wondering what God was saying to Isaiah and what he meant by all the symbolism and metaphors, it has been translated into a personal promise from God directly to me! It is now so absolutely clear to me that my life and the journey I have been on has been purposed for my specific calling to rescue those living in the wasteland and guide them back home to the garden where we as children of God are meant to live here on earth.

What amazes me most is how clearly and beautifully God opened my eyes to the call on my life by translating these verses into a personal dialogue and with such precise clarity He spells out why He chose me and what He is about to do.

To Look at Dario 41:8-20 closely, God starts out by stating that I belong to him and this gives me such a sense of security. He then confirms that He has given me the gift of brokenness and that is was not an accident or punishment; brokenness is one of the greatest gifts a believer can receive. God breaks deeply those He uses greatly! He then says that because I have suffered so much and have been deeply broken that my life will be a huge example of His restorative power to rescue the destitute. He handpicked me because He believed in me; that makes me feel loved beyond measure. He loved me the most when I was farthest away, a picture of the depth of God's empathy towards His children. And since He called me to this assignment there is no need for me to be afraid. God never calls us to something that He won't fully protect and provide for us. He even warns anyone who would think of messing with me and my calling to be aware for they will suffer greatly if they try and interfere. He then gives me a new name, "Affectionate One!" It says it in verse 14, "You are my affectionate one!" Do you know that is what my mom used to refer to me as; her affectionate one! I would often listen to her introduce me and tell someone about me and say, "Dario is my affectionate one" He always gives a hug and kiss and tells me that he loves me. I love doing that to PAPA as well!!!

God then goes on to inform me that He has equipped me with His powerful Spirit and I have become an instrument to crush the Enemy of the wasteland known as self-love. It is self-love that keeps souls trapped in the wasteland and my mission statement is to rescue those very souls. Self-love comes from rebellion towards God and the love of this world. But despite their rebellion and misplaced love God has a plan to rescue them and lead them to the garden; to transform their lives. We are literally drawing them a map with instructions! Pretty cool! God then closes out with a promise that this rescue mission is so grand and masterful that anyone who has eyes to see will know beyond a shadow of a doubt that only God could have done this!

To sum up the call that has been placed on my life I would use the term 'written in stone on the tablet of my heart'. There is no possible way I can doubt what God has called me to. He has explained to me the first 45 years of my life which I in lived in a cave in the wasteland of this world. Though it was miserable I was never in danger. He had my back the entire time, as well as a plan to rescue me, restore me and set me free in the garden. If that doesn't give me a sense of God's omnipotence then nothing will. I always wondered why life made no sense until now. I was looking at it through a set of worldly eyes. But in the garden I have new eyes, the eyes of God and a perspective to see as He sees. It's like the difference between seeing the world through the eyes of a caterpillar, then being transformed to see as the butterfly sees. But also to move about as swiftly and freely as the butterfly does with its beautiful, extremely soft and yet strong set of wings. The butterfly looks so peaceful and free as it moves throughout the air being admired by all. That is exactly how God wants the world to view His children because that is our inheritance here on earth.

We are not supposed to moping around in the dark claiming 'woe is me!' We were meant for more, for life and freedom to enjoy this life as a glimpse of eternity. We are not in eternity yet, but we will one day, "For now we see only a reflection as in a mirror; then we shall see face to face. Now I know in part; then I shall know fully, even as I am fully known." (1ˢᵗ Corinthians 13:12) I don't know about you, but I want to have the most amazing glimpse of eternity before I go home to heaven and experience the real thing. Don't you? Don't you want to wake up every morning and read a love letter from God in your own personal dialogue straight out of the bible? I do! Don't you want to walk step by step with God, Jesus and the Holy Spirit every single second of every day? I do! Don't you want to pinch yourself every day to make sure you aren't in a dream because life is so amazing living in the garden here on earth? I do! I believe everyone wants that unless they have allowed themselves to be deceived or are afraid to make the journey. Either way, God and I are coming after you. We won't leave you behind. If you are apprehensive we will wait patiently for you. If you are ready to be transformed, come' on. If you are scared; we will hold your hand. In Dario 41:9 God says, "I traveled that far to retrieve you and rescue you and I am never going to stop." He won't ever give up on YOU!!!

Since the moment I got the call to enter the garden at 12:49 a.m. on November 28ᵗʰ my life has flowed from one glimpse of eternity to the next; from 'glory to glory.' Now I want to go back to the wasteland as a bridge guide, look the Enemy in the face and say "let my people go!" No more sitting there till you die, time to get up and a start your journey home!

Look! Papa, Jesus, the Holy Spirit and I have drawn you a map! We lived and walked it out together. My blood, sweat and tears are all over it. We want to help you all live the best life possible here on earth and carry it into eternity. Please say yes to your personal Psalm 23 journey; the one God has uniquely designed for you and you alone. It's yours to take and experience to the fullest. Please don't be afraid, procrastinate or walk away; you will regret it for the rest of your days on earth and in eternity. Please say yes and watch God restore your life. You will never regret it!

See you all in the Garden! - D

END OF BOOK

CPSIA information can be obtained
at www.ICGtesting.com
Printed in the USA
LVHW092229080120
643030LV00001B/179/P